BUTTERED SIDE DOWN

BUTTERED
SIDE DOWN
A SLICE OF COUNTRY LIFE

Faith Addis

Published by BBC Worldwide Limited,
80 Wood Lane, London W12 0TT
First published by André Deutsch Limited 1985
This edition first published 2000

Reprinted 2000

ISBN 0 563 53725 6

Commissioning Editor: Emma Shackleton
Project Editor: Anthony Brennan

Set in Berling by Keystroke
Printed and bound in Great Britain by Mackays of Chatham
Cover printed by Belmont Press Limited, Northampton

To Esther

Foreword

Looking back to the 1970s which is when my books began, I realise how lucky we were to be able to do the things we did. Nowadays there are so many regulations strangling small enterprises you probably need a degree in form-filling to start a flower farm or a children's holiday home, to name just two of our ventures.

Lots of our projects could have been done more efficiently or profitably but that's easy to say now. I expect everyone feels the same with the benefit of hindsight. But when you're young and full of ideas and energy, being sensible doesn't come into it. You tend to say yes to everything. At any rate that's what we did and we enjoyed ourselves no end despite the ever-present overdraft.

One of our favourite memories is that of the anemone crop. Having back-achingly sown them, grown them and weeded them, we planned to pick the first flush in tight bud ready for sale. However the flowers had other ideas and shot into full bloom two days before they were supposed to. This meant that they were unsaleable. But the sight of a flower field vibrant with colour from end to end more than made up for a few pounds' loss.

Then came the books and the hundreds of letters I received from people who enjoyed sharing our country living vicariously. I am so pleased that with the re-issue of the books another generation can share the ups and downs of being smallholders. And to those who have written to ask 'What happened next?' Well, not a lot really. Having moved house six times in twenty years we came to the conclusion that we were getting too long in the tooth to keep doing up houses and gardens, so we have taken root in a quiet village where we have just one acre to tend. We have not 'moved with the times' and don't intend to.

No computer, no digital this or electronic that. (Getting the laundry scrubbed on stones at the river's edge can get tough in winter but we Luddites have our standards.)

The children sneakily grew up when we weren't looking and are now, hard to believe, in their forties. Sara has provided two grandchildren while Marcus continues to travel the world living out of a rucksack.

Faith Addis, 2000

Chapter One

Sometimes, just sometimes when it's 6.30 a.m. in January, and your circulation is bypassing your fingers and toes, you do tend to wonder what it was that made you move to the country. Most people are a bit snappy on cold mornings and Brian and I are no exceptions. This particular January dawn started with a difference of opinion over icicles.

Personally, I like icicles. I like the tinkly noise they make when you run your nail along them, and I couldn't understand why Brian was so cross when I pointed out a beautiful cluster. Admittedly, they were in a place where you would not normally expect to find icicles, namely inside our bedroom window, and perhaps it had not been very tactful of me to wake him up at 6.30 to admire them, but I thought he might show *some* interest.

'Interest? Are you stark staring mad? They're *inside*. We've been sleeping all night under a glacier and you expect me to *admire* them?' There was quite a lot more in this vein, then he sat up in bed and switched on his bedside light. 'Oh, no,' he moaned, and slid back under the bedclothes, 'please let me be dreaming. Please don't let there be snow on the bed and a lunatic wife when I wake up.'

'The wind must have changed in the night,' I said, poking my finger in the layer of snow on the windowsill. 'We'll have to move the bed away from the window.'

Brian muttered something about moving to Africa, and pulled the snow-encrusted blankets tightly round his shoulders. This left me with no blankets, so I got up, and gasped as the cold air hit my skin. 'I'll make some tea,' I said.

'Never mind tea. Make some curtains.'

'Do you want yours up here?'

'No, I don't feel safe with that avalanche creeping towards me.'

We put on our dressing-gowns and made for the sitting-room where last night's log fire was soon persuaded into life again. The dogs came out of their baskets and hogged the hearthrug, while Small perched on the arm of Brian's chair and purred.

'This is more like it,' Brian said. 'Perhaps we could sleep down here for the rest of the winter.'

'I'll make some bedroom curtains,' I said. We had been in the house only a few weeks and had been too busy seeing to the farm animals' comforts to pay much attention to our own.

It was a large, draughty, inconvenient house, with too many passages and stairs – but apart from that, it was all right. It had been built about the time of Henry VIII, when serfs were two a groat and wouldn't have dared to complain about a few icicles in their bedroom. Brian and I occupied a converted dairy wing, and Anne, my mother, the main part of the house. Each half was completely self-contained, with its own kitchen, bathroom, sitting-rooms and several big bedrooms. There was rather too much house, even for dual occupation, but, like a lot of big houses in Devon, it had been relatively cheap.

Our main interest was in the 20 acres that went with it – acres that we fondly imagined would earn us a living. Brian planned to grow things – he had not yet decided what – and I was going to start a riding stables. In our spare time we would breed pedigree Gloucester Old Spot pigs for fun. Even we knew that pigs are a smallholder's least profitable line.

'Come on, it's getting light.' Brian forced himself to leave the fire. The people on the *Today* programme kept telling us what the time was in that maddeningly cheerful way they go in for first thing in the morning. They seemed to know there was a cow to be milked, hungry animals to feed and frozen troughs to thaw.

Once outside, of course, it was fine. Not literally – the wind was blowing powdered snow in one ear and out the other – but once we started work, we were soon glowing. We carried gallons of hot water out first and thawed the water buckets, then we fed the ponies, rabbits and poultry. Elizabeth, the Jersey house cow, was Brian's favourite and he usually milked her while I saw to my own favourites, the pigs.

For the time being we were using a row of stables to house the pigs as there hadn't yet been time to fix up an electrically fenced paddock for them. Keeping pigs indoors has two advantages: (a) the person feeding them stays warm and dry, and (b) the pigs' paddock gets a rest from delving noses. But neither of these compensates the pig itself for its loss of freedom, and our outdoor-reared sows didn't like the new arrangements one bit. We gave them all old tyres to play with and fresh branches to gnaw; the young weaners soon adapted to confinement, but the sows never stopped grumbling.

I opened the first door and rattled the feed bucket. 'Wakey wakey, girls, good morning.' Bramble and Briar grunted like teenagers and burrowed deeper into their straw. I tipped the pig nuts into their trough. 'You can stop sulking and get up. I can't help the weather, can I? Anyway, it's much worse in Scotland; they've got blizzards up there and all the roads are blocked.' Bramble and Briar heaved themselves out of bed. While they were eating, I fluffed up their bed with a pitchfork and added some fresh straw. Phyllis, Rose and Rose Hip in the next stable snuffled impatiently under their door. Was I going to be all day in there? Some people have been up for *hours* and how about some breakfast? That started the weaners off, and anyone who has heard hungry piglets screaming for room service will know what that sounds like.

I quickly fed the other sows before starting the baby feeds. The noise level grew and I pulled my anorak hood over my ears. '*Shut up* the lot of you,' I yelled. They stopped. Like puppies, they will pause to draw breath once they're sure you have taken their orders. Hurriedly, I tipped milk and cereal into their trough and stood aside as twelve fat little torpedoes fought to be first to get at it. As they happily slurped up Elizabeth's rich milk, I walked round them, inspecting each one closely for physical well-being. In textbooks this is called good husbandry, but I call it sheer pleasure.

The sound of an approaching radio made me leap for a broom and shovel. Brian's radio is his life-support system. When I divorce him, I'm going to cite Radio 4 as the other party, particularly Alistair Cook and *Woman's Hour*. On the other hand, the ever-present radio does provide me with an early-warning system, and he hardly ever catches me out.

He put the milk in the porch to cool and came over to the stables. 'All done?' he said.

'Nearly. I'll just finish mucking out and I'll be in.' (Finish? I hadn't even started.) Fortunately pigs leave their places as they would like to find them, neatly divided into sleeping, eating and dunging areas, so it never takes very long to sweep up their droppings.

Anne was up and pottering in her kitchen when we went indoors. She was dressed in thin slacks and a T-shirt and looked several years my junior. 'Hello, you've finished early,' she said.

'We woke up early. It was too cold to stay in bed.'

'Cold? I was just thinking how lucky we are here. It said on the news they've got blocked roads and blizzards in the north.' She opened her back door and looked up at the sky. 'Do you think we'll get snow?'

'Look down a bit,' I suggested. 'That white stuff all over the garden...'

'Oh, *that*,' she said airily, 'just a sprinkle.' She came back inside, leaving the back door wide open. I'm convinced my mother was a polar bear in her last life; she never feels the cold and never shuts doors. I shivered and sat on the edge of the Aga. 'Have you unpacked your sewing-machine yet? I must make some curtains today and I can't remember where we put mine.'

'You'll get piles if you sit there. I'll do your curtains for you. Last time you borrowed my machine it took me half an hour to readjust the tension *and* you bent one of the bobbins.'

'I didn't think you could bend bobbins.'

'You can bend anything if you force it in with a screwdriver. Which room do you want curtains for?'

'All of them,' I said promptly. If she was in a curtain-making mood, it seemed a waste not to have the lot done. 'And a new coat for old Honey, please. The one I made her won't stay on properly.'

'I'm not surprised if you made it. I see poor Brian is held together with Copydex again. Don't you ever sew buttons on?'

I didn't like the way the conversation was going, so I slid off the Aga and went to fetch Honey in for her fitting.

'Bring them all in,' Anne called after me. 'I've made myself too much porridge.'

Our three dogs, Honey, Parsley and Ella, were great friends with Anne's two, Inky and Melly. They never quarelled, not even on bone days, although they would put up a token show of possession if their own bone was a particularly choice one. It was a good job that they did get on because our cats didn't, and it would have driven us all potty to have two warring species under the same roof.

While the dogs were eating their porridge Anne measured Honey. '28-16-15,' she said. 'Write that down, would you?'

'Which bit is the 16?'

'Shoulder to tail. What colour would she like this time?'

'Something that can be seen a long way off. Then, if she loses it, we've got some chance of finding it.'

'She won't lose it. I'll do it with Velcro fastenings.'

'You won't forget the curtains, will you?' I said anxiously. 'We can always wrap Honey in an old sweater, but our bedroom is letting in snow.'

'You should double-glaze it. I've done mine.'

'You've what?'

'The rain came in. Rather annoying. There was a damp patch on my carpet. So I double-glazed the windows. Come and see.'

We went upstairs, picking our way carefully round a mountain of spare furniture on the landing. 'Must get it into a home,' Anne murmured vaguely, as if referring to an ageing relative. She has been collecting furniture since the year dot and can't bear to part with anything.

The double-glazing was simple but effective. 'I didn't bother with battens and all that nonsense,' Anne said. 'I think they make it sound complicated in magazines just to fill up space. All you do is hold the polythene taut over the window frame and hammer it in. Double the edges back over, tack it all round and it's done.'

'It's brilliant,' I said. 'Where did you get this heavy-duty polythene?'

'I stole it from Harrods. You remember that Bergère suite I bought in their fire-damage sale?'

'No.'

'Well, it was about 1964, I think. Anyway, they delivered it wrapped in 6-foot-wide polythene and the rest of the roll sort of fell off the back of their van. I gave the man ten bob.'

By nightfall, our draughty Tudor pile was hermetically sealed, courtesy of Harrods, with beautifully made curtains acting as long-stops. Honey, the old mongrel, was the proud possessor of a yellow-and-brown-striped coat with Velcro fastenings, and we all slept soundly, confident that spring couldn't be far off.

Indeed, it did seem that, for once, the weather would be kind. The West Country escaped the January blizzards that were paralyzing the northern half of Britain, and the sprinkling of snow that fell in Devon was soon washed away by rain.

Blissfully unaware of what was going to happen on 16 February (the Met. men were awfully good at keeping secrets), Brian and I set up the smallholding. The pigs, to their relief, were moved out of the stables and into a 3-acre orchard next to the house, and the ponies, to *their* relief, were able to spend the cold nights under cover. 'Native ponies,' said my pony-management manual, 'will be perfectly happy to live outdoors in all weathers.' Well, some might, but for mine the highlight of their day was to be first in the stampede to get into a nice, dry stable, and I had several bruised toenails to prove it.

We reassembled the rabbits' winter quarters, a large wooden hut we had brought with us from the last house, and put the rabbits in loose. They had the freedom of the whole hut, but if they wanted privacy, they could retire to their open-fronted hutches, which were placed in a row on bricks along one wall. This is called a 'colony' system and is much frowned upon by modern rabbit-breeders. They claim it encourages cross-infection, but in our experience it is caged animals that get ill. We found the colony system labour-saving and humane; there are few prettier sights than a litter of baby rabbits playing, and few more pathetic than a row of rabbit faces behind bars.

Poultry next. Brian towed the hen-house behind the tractor and positioned it in the pigs' orchard. We didn't want the

14

chickens to be too free-ranging – they tended to use the hay-barn as a lavatory if given the choice – so we fenced round their house with ten 6-foot portable hurdles. This gave them enough space for the time being, and could be moved along on to fresh grass when necessary. The Muscovy ducks we left to their own devices; they paddled around in the many small streams that bounded our fields and came into a barn at night. We clipped their wings to stop them flying away, and were pleased to note that it also stopped them roosting in high places – duck muck is quite difficult stuff to wash out of your hair.

Brian booked a contractor to plough a few acres for the proposed commercial produce, and another contractor with a JCB digger to unclog some badly neglected ditches. While they were there, he asked them to plough an extra half-acre next to the house, which we would later use as a vegetable garden. The place hummed with activity; Brian hired a rotovator and followed the plough, turning the coarse tilth into a slightly less coarse tilth. (January isn't really the best time to do this sort of thing, but Brian was too impatient to wait.) Then, with a friend's help, he built a stock-proof fence around the new garden.

He also bought a hand-propelled seeder, an ingenious machine that was supposed to take the guesswork out of seed-sowing. You fill its belly with, say, turnip seeds, and as you push it along the row, it drops one seed every 6 inches. As if this weren't clever enough, it also covers the seeds it has sown *and* marks out a parallel groove in the soil for the next row. It worked beautifully on our sitting-room carpet, and if you want a turnip crop in your carpet, I can thoroughly recommend it. In the initial 'field trials', however, it showed a marked dislike of stones and mud, and would spit out seeds only if one of us (me) walked in front of it raking stones out of its path. When I was on speaking terms with Brian again (nothing brings me to the boil faster than having to be subservient to a *machine*), he said it would work perfectly in the spring when the soil would be more friable. He had to say that because he had spent £250 on it, and all he'd had back was an enraged wife and a sitting-room carpet full of grooves.

His side of the smallholding done for the time being, we

started on mine, the riding business. Brian turned part of one of the barns into a tack room for me. It was a good place to be on a wet day, dark and warm and smelling of leather. It had been cart-horse stalls in the olden days, and still had the original cobbled floor and deep wooden mangers. The oak partitions had been worn smooth by four hundred years of sweaty bodies, and even I, who am about as psychic as a plate of porridge, could feel the presence of those hardworking, bygone farm horses – shires, judging by the height of the hay racks. I think they would have approved of the way Brian had renovated their old home.

Approval of a different sort was the next objective. There are lots of rules and regulations to be complied with before you can get a licence to open a riding school, rightly so in our opinion. But the forms: no wonder the trees are disappearing at such a rate.

You start by filling in one form, nice and clearly so that they (the Planning Dept) can photocopy it and give a copy to all the other departments involved. But the other departments – Health, Veterinary and Fire – won't play unless they have their own forms, handwritten and signed by you, the applicant. So you, the applicant, with much grinding of teeth, fill in three more forms identical to the first one. These four forms provide two pairs for the Town Hall to breed from. And it's no use getting shirty at this point or they'll lose all your forms and make you start again. So you wait. And wait.

During the waiting period, I reviewed the workers, the ponies that were going to earn me £2 an hour once we were all legal. There was Monty, a 14.2 black cob, always calm and a steadying influence on his best friend, Wellington, a Welsh grey, born in June and a true Gemini. Someone else's grass always looked greener to him. He was the champion breaker-out, champion fidget and had the kindest, friendliest nature imaginable.

Next (in order of height) was Noah, an Exmoor cross saint, only 12.2, but the brains of the herd. I am Noah's slave. He has me in the palm of his hoof, and if I had to choose between husband, children and Noah, it would be a close-run thing.

Lastly, little Rocky, a black Shetland, who should have been called Billy Bunter. On the rare occasions when he wasn't eating, he was teasing the others, trying to get them to play with him. He was only five, and his youthful high spirits often earned him a nip from his elders, which is how it should be.

(There was a fifth, a robot-like pony called Owen, who was such a goody goody that he was no fun to ride. The other ponies didn't much like him either, so I sold him to a woman who wanted a safe pony for her grandchildren.)

'Four,' said Tony, our friend and farrier, 'isn't enough. You'll need at least six and preferably ten.'

'We can't afford any more at the moment,' I said. 'Later, maybe, if it gets busy, I'll think about buying a couple more. I want to start small. Don't forget, I'm a complete beginner in this business. I couldn't handle more than four on my own.'

'There'll be girls,' Tony said.

'Girls?'

'Girls. Wherever there are ponies, you get girls. God knows where they come from – they just appear. You'll have so many helpers you'll be turning them away.' Tony and his wife had a riding school themselves, but he was very generous in his support for mine. He said the competition would drum up business for both, and as it turned out he was right.

'But I can't *depend* on girls materializing, Tony,' I objected. 'Brian will be too busy to help me. I think I'd better stick at four for now.'

But in the horse world, empty paddocks have a way of attracting would-be grazers, and during the next few weeks I was offered (by complete strangers) two Arab mares as an outright gift and no fewer than five thoroughbred horses from separate owners who wanted to loan them out for the summer. I was tempted by the Arabs, until Tony put me off by telling me how thin-skinned they were, always needing a warm rug when there was a nip in the air. I wouldn't have had any of the thoroughbreds as a gift, though, because their slave mentality makes me sad. What *intelligent* animal would let itself be conned into jumping a 7-foot wall just so that its owner can win a silver cup?

No, it had to be ponies or nothing, and anyone over 10 stone could be passed on to Tony, who had some big horses. In return, I hoped he would send me some of his smaller clients – the three- and four-year-olds whom he sometimes regarded as a waste of time because they needed individual supervision.

Then, in February, just as the first primroses were appearing, we heard of a horse and pony in urgent need of a temporary home. Their owners, an army family, were being posted, and the friends who had been looking after the horse and pony were themselves moving house shortly and couldn't keep them. I liked the sound of both animals and agreed to have them on loan.

They were in Wales, a round trip of some 350 miles, which Tony, who was going to transport them, said would take about eight or nine hours on a fine day. I set out with him one bright morning at 8 a.m. assuring Brian that, barring punctures, we should be back before dark.

When we got to the Severn Bridge, it was swaying around like mad in a gale-force wind had suddenly sprung up, and the man on the toll-gate said we would be daft to try to get across in an unladen horsebox. I agreed with him wholeheartedly, but Tony said he hadn't come all this way just to turn back.

He put the engine into first gear and drove on to the bridge. The sensation was nightmarish. The bridge was going sideways and so was the horsebox, creaking and straining as it took the force of the wind. Tony gripped the steering wheel tightly and stayed in first gear, coaxing the lorry forward at about 10 mph. When we got to the middle, things became very dodgy indeed. I heard Tony say, 'Wind your window down – quick,' and the calm, authoritative way he said it made me obey instantly. He wound his down too and a wind such as I've never known before and never want to know again, whooshed through the cab. Tony shouted above the noise: 'If she goes over, jump out. Understand?' I nodded dumbly and concentrated on wondering why some men call their vehicles 'she'. It was better than wondering what it was going to feel like when we drowned in the foaming River Severn hundreds of feet below us.

Chapter Two

We didn't drown. We reached the other side physically intact and only one of us a nervous wreck. Tony parked the lorry in a lay-by. It gave a great hiss of relief. I needed more than a hiss, and tried to unscrew the lid of the coffee flask but it wouldn't budge.

'Give it here,' Tony said, 'you're a bit cold.' It seemed rather an understatement to describe someone with rigor mortis. We sipped the hot coffee and watched the eastbound traffic forming a queue up to the bridge, which now had a BRIDGE CLOSED sign up. It turned out that we had been the last to cross.

'Why did you have to have the windows open?' I said, when at last I discovered I could still speak.

'It cuts down the wind resistance on the sides of the cab. If the wind can go through, there's less chance of it blowing the thing over. It'll be easier going back though: the weight of the horses will steady the box.'

'Going *back*? I'm not going back.'

Tony ignored this and started the engine. 'Best get on,' he said. 'Looks like snow ahead.' We went past Abergavenny and up into the hills, where there was a thin layer of snow on the iced roads. It hardly seemed possible that not four hours ago we had left a garden full of early primroses. I felt in some way responsible for the weather, and rather guilty about the whole trip, especially when we had to stop twice to clear a way for the horsebox. Driving a huge vehicle on a good day is quite an art – the driver has to be aware of the width of the road ahead and the head-room under trees – but on a bad day on strange roads you really need someone walking in front with a red flag.

Eventually, we found the hill farm where we were to collect the horses, and were welcomed in and thawed out by the couple who were boarding them. They were surprised we had set out in such weather and urged us to get back as quickly as possible because the one o'clock forecast had been bad. By three o'clock we were on the road again with our two passengers contentedly chomping hay in the back. There hadn't been much time to examine them when we were loading, but they seemed fine; Rebel was about 16 hands, chestnut, and wore a New Zealand rug, while Jinks, a Welsh grey, looked identical to Wellington.

Tony drove slowly and carefully back to the Severn Bridge, which was now open again. Here he got out to pat and reassure the horses, telling them how brave they were being and that they would soon be home. I could have done with some reassurance too, but as I wasn't a horse, I didn't get it.

The return crossing was easier and, once over, we headed home quickly. Brian met us at the gate with a torch and helped to unload the horses. He was very surprised to hear about the snow. It had been clear and sunny all day at home and he hadn't even needed a coat.

Sarah, the seven-year-old daughter of our friends Valerie and George who were staying with us at the time, had hoped she would be able to see the new horses arriving, but we were so late back that she had had to go to bed.

'She's not asleep, though,' Valerie said. 'I heard her get out of bed when she heard the horsebox coming.'

'I'll go and say goodnight,' I said, and went upstairs.

'I'm not asleep,' Sarah called when she heard me tiptoeing along the landing. I went in and sat on her bed. 'Sorry to be so late, Sarah. We had to drive slowly so that the horses didn't feel sick.'

'Ooh, you smell *lovely*. Can I borrow your gloves for tonight, please? I'll put them under the pillow and dream about horses. What are they like? Can I ride them tomorrow?'

You can ride the grey one; he's called Jinks and he's the same size as Wellington. But the other one, Rebel, is too big for you.'

'He'll do for Mummy then. She's put on a lot of weight, hasn't she?'

'You're not exactly wasting away yourself.' We chatted a while, then I stood up. 'I must go. I haven't had my dinner yet and I want to have a bath first.'

'*Want* a bath?' Sarah said. (She was the most intelligent child Brian and I had ever known, but she had the normal seven-year-old's mistrust of soap and water.)

'Yes. I'm stiff with cold. It was snowing in Wales.'

A most peculiar look flitted across her face, a sort of 'I've got a secret' look. Then she buried her face in my horsy gloves and said something I couldn't hear.

'Goodnight then, horrible. See you in the morning.'

'Night. Thanks for the gloves.'

The next morning, 16 February, we all overslept. It was as cold as it had been in Wales yesterday, with the unmistakable taste of snow in the air, confirmed by the weather forecast and the lunatic behaviour of the cats and dogs. We were late finishing the morning chores as we had spent quite a long time watching the ponies getting to know their new companions. Young Sarah seemed quite happy to sit on a gate giving a running commentary on which pony was doing what, so we decided to postpone her ride until after lunch. Looking back, it seems incredible that five reasonably intelligent adults, all of whom had heard the weather forecast, spent the morning casually sweeping the yard and admiring the ponies. At noon Brian suggested that he and George nip into town to buy fish and chips for lunch. Valerie and I knew this meant a quiet pint at the pub first, and asked them to try to be back by 1.30 so that Sarah could get in her ride. They drove off and we went indoors to have a coffee with Anne, leaving Sarah outside with the ponies.

A short while later a small snowman appeared at the kitchen door. Valerie let out a shriek that must have been heard in Taunton and leapt to her feet. 'Sarah!'

'The snow's come,' Sarah said calmly. 'I knew it would. I wished it.'

'Then you can bloody well *un*wish it,' Valerie snapped, and rushed outside. 'Oh, my God, we've got a plane to catch on Friday and the dentist in London on Thursday.' Her voice trailed off when she reached the garden. Anne lifted one of the cats off the Aga and handed it to Sarah. 'Dry your hair,' she said vaguely, and followed Valerie out.

It was an awesome sight, the first of many that week. Already the ground was covered in an inch of snow, but it was the snowflakes themselves that were so breathtaking. They were huge, some as big as the palms of our hands, and coming down at such a rate that as we watched, small plants disappeared, the wheelbarrow filled and the garden bench turned white.

I fetched a camera, and it's an indication of how dark it was that even though there was a medium-fast film in it and I opened up to 4.5, I still couldn't get a reading off the sky. It was quite eerie not being able to see as far as the end of the stable block some 50 yards away. Everything was so quiet and still – no wind, no distant traffic, nothing except this silent smothering of the landscape.

'What's the time?' said Valerie.

'Nearly one. Better get some plates in the oven, George and Brian will have started back by now.'

Luckily for them they had. If they had left it another half-hour, they would have had to walk.

'Good job you went to Wales yesterday,' they said, handing over six parcels of fish and chips. 'Who would have thought that this much could fall in an hour?' Sarah confessed that she was responsible. 'I wished it,' she said. 'I've never seen snow before, so I wished and wished that it would snow on this leave.' She had been globe-trotting with her parents since she was a baby, first when George's job took them to Spain, then to Algeria, where, as Sarah said, all you get is boring old sun every day.

During the afternoon, the snow eased off, leaving about 4 inches lying. Sarah's ride had to be abandoned, but she was very good about it and helped me to get the ponies in early instead, riding Rocky bareback from the paddock to the stable, then rubbing him dry with straw. The evening weather forecast said there was more snow to come. What it didn't say was how much more.

We were woken up next morning by the sound of Valerie having hysterics in the next bedroom. We both guessed the cause, shot out of bed and pulled back the curtains. People say 'I couldn't believe my eyes' and it doesn't mean much until it happens to be literally true. The sight that met our unbelieving eyes was a snowscape where the only recognizable feature was an electricity pylon about half a mile away. The rest was a solid block of white. Up against one side of the house the snow had drifted to about 15 feet, completely obliterating the ground-floor windows and doors. I felt as though a giant hand was squeezing my stomach and I saw by Brian's face that he was thinking what I was thinking.

'The pigs,' I whispered. 'Oh, my poor, poor pigs.' I stumbled towards the door.

'Wait,' Brian said. 'Dress first. We won't be able to help them if we get frozen stiff.' We pulled on sweaters and trousers and ran downstairs. On opening the front door (the side opposite the 15-foot drift), our first problem was to overcome a strong desire to shut it again. The snow in the small, walled front garden was 3 feet deep, higher than the garden wall and beyond that it had drifted even higher. We made our way with difficulty to where we guessed the gate to be and walked over.

'Spades,' Brian said. 'Oh hell, they're inside the feed room, aren't they?'

The feed room was a disused stable with the normal outward-opening divided doors. We worked our way across the yard; it was like moving in a dream, having to lift one leg with both hands, then going back for the other leg and hanging on to the boot so as not to leave it behind in the snow. George followed in our path and the three of us reached the feed room and scraped away with our gloved hands until we found the top door bolt. It was on a level with our knees and opened easily. Brian slithered through, jumped down inside and handed out spades and shovels before climbing out again. The ponies whickered their morning welcome and kicked their doors in anticipation of breakfast.

It didn't take long to clear a patch outside the feed room and open the lower door, but it did feel strange to stand at ground level enclosed in a pen of snow up to our shoulders. We could see Anne and Valerie in the porch remonstrating with an invisible Sarah who had evidently set out down the garden path in our tracks.

'Can you chuck us some shovels?' Valerie called. 'Sarah's up to her chin already.'

'I'll go,' George said, and retraced his steps to the house using two spades like ski sticks.

Brian filled two buckets with pig nuts. 'Why bother?' I said bitterly. 'They'll be dead by now. I'll never forgive myself. If only we'd kept them in until spring. If only...'

'*Shut up.*' Brian handed me a bucket. 'Walk behind me and put your feet in my footsteps, it'll make it easier.' He looped his bucket over the spade handle and started forward with the spade over his shoulder.

In order to get to the pigs' orchard, we had to make our way down the drive – about 50 yards – then turn right outside the gate and go a further 30 yards along the road. It took us nearly an hour to reach the area where we knew the pigs' arks were, an hour of scrambling through snow that in places had drifted to 12 feet and more, higher than the hedges. The snow was like feathers – dry and soft and very difficult to get a grip on.

We got there at last and Brian started digging. As we had only one spade, I broke a branch off a tree and used it as a probe. Immediately it hit a corrugated iron roof – Brian had guessed our position right and was digging down to a pig. I banged the branch as hard as I could on to the iron roof. *Rose Hip answered.*

'It's Rose Hip!' I yelled, scrabbling the snow away with my hands.

'You can't *possibly* know which one it is.'

'Why not? You can tell Marcus and Sara apart, can't you?'

'I doubt I could under 6 feet of snow.'

We dug and scraped until at last we uncovered the entrance of an ark and pulled aside the sacking draught excluder. Rose Hip poked her face out. She was warm and well but, she indicated, starving. Brian climbed up the snow and handed down a bucket of nuts. 'Tip some out on the snow,' he said.

'We might not be able to get water to them for ages, but she'll get some moisture this way.'

While she ate, we uncovered the next ark, Rosie and Phyll's. Even Brian couldn't mistake Phyll's bossy tones, and he dug away vigorously, guided by her shrill complaints: Was this our idea of a joke? Didn't we know what the time was? Some people should try being buried alive themselves, see how *they* like it. Brian made them a slightly bigger dugout than Rose Hip's as there were two of them, and threw their nuts down quickly to shut them up.

Bramble and Briar had not fared as well as the others because their ark was a lot smaller. When we got to them, they were in a deep sleep and their skins had turned a funny colour. We hauled them out on to the snow and slapped them like newborn babies. Once they had some fresh air into their lungs they were fine, somewhat mystified at finding themselves walled in on three sides but none the worse for their narrow escape.

All the piglets were alive and well. We hadn't really worried about them since their house was a converted deep-litter poultry-house made of wood, and had a steep, ventilated roof. But there was a different problem here: the piglets were too young to be left without actual water, so after emptying the feed buckets into their hopper, we made our laborious way to the stream that ran through the orchard.

It was like fairyland down there. The fast-flowing water had cut amazing patterns into the snow and left overhanging crystals of ice, which sparkled blue and green, and even red where it reflected off coloured pebbles in the stream. But we hadn't time to linger. By now Elizabeth was mooing her head off. 'Poor thing, she must be bursting,' Brian said. 'I'd better get back.'

'I'll come too. I need grain for the chickens and some more buckets for the pigs' water – they'll never make it to the stream.'

Going back was much easier because we weren't carrying anything and suddenly we began to enjoy the day. Maybe it was a reaction after the worry of not knowing if the pigs had suffocated, but I think it was the sheer beauty of the snow.

We met the dogs in what was normally the gateway, crazy with excitement at being able to walk straight on to the cowshed roof. Small, who thinks she is a dog, wanted to join in the game, but she evidently didn't care for the feel of the snow too much, and kept shaking her front paws one at a time to keep them dry.

We waved to Anne, George and Valerie and shouted that the pigs were OK. They had been doing sterling work in the yard while we had been away, cutting slit trenches outside each stable so that the doors would open, and relaying hot water from the house to thaw the troughs. George had dragged a bale of hay from the top of the stack – the only hay visible in the open-fronted barn was the top layer – and divided it between the five ponies and Rebel.

'I didn't know what to give Elizabeth, so I left her,' he said. 'She's been mooing for half an hour.'

'I'd better milk her,' said Brian, and moved towards the house.

'You don't need to go indoors, Brian,' Valerie said. 'We put your milking bucket outside Elizabeth's pen to save you a double journey.'

'That was nice of you, Val, but I must warm my hands first.'

'Well,' said Valerie in astonishment, 'I do think that's *gallant* of you, Brian. I hope Elizabeth appreciates it.'

Brian roared with laughter and explained that it was not so much for Elizabeth's comfort as his own. 'I wouldn't be able to milk with numb fingers,' he said. 'And anyway, I wouldn't without washing first. You have to be very careful with raw milk.'

It was lunchtime before all the animals and poultry had been seen to, and would have been later still without the extra muscle of our visitors. Wearily we came indoors, stripped off our soaking clothes and left them to drip on the flagstone floor in the hall. Hot soup and dry socks restored our spirits in no time, as did the phone calls from family and friends in London, who had already seen the one o'clock news on TV and couldn't believe it. We described everything in detail and they oohed and aahed in all the right places and offered to send books and chocolate. Quite how the postman was going to deliver these survival aids nobody knew, but it was a cheering thought.

Next we tried some phoning round to our fellow smallholders. In most cases the lines were down, but the ones who did answer reported similar conditions to our own – deep drifts, confused animals and numb hands and feet. One, who had a small flock of sheep, had heeded last night's forecast and put them in a barn for the night. The barn roof had collapsed under the weight of the snow, but the sheep had had the sense to take cover under a hay wagon and were all alive. Our friend had hauled them out one at a time and, as all her outbuildings were occupied, had taken them into the house, but now her grandmother had locked herself in the lavatory and was refusing to come out until the sheep were removed from the dining-room.

But for sheer resourcefulness it would be hard to beat the man who, seeing heavy snow on the way, and unable to house his flock of sheep, drove them into a quiet country lane and blocked off either end. All night long he walked them up and down, backwards and forwards. By morning the snow had formed a roof overhead across the bordering hedges and the sheep were safe on flat-packed snow below. His family dug their way to him and made a track so that he could take fodder to the flock.

It was Tony, though, who had the most hair-raising story to tell. His holding was up in the hills, so had caught the worst of the snow, and it had taken him an hour to reach the roof of the stables, and then a lot of false starts before he located a skylight. Not wishing to be entombed with the horses, he tied rope round the waist of his five-year-old son, Raymond, and lowered him down inside. Like most country boys Raymond was extremely practical and was able to follow Tony's instructions and feed the horses. Now it was mid-afternoon and the family had just finished digging a trench to the stable entrance.

Before ringing off Tony gave me a very important piece of advice: 'Cut your ponies' rations down to almost nothing,' he said. 'They're not using any energy shut up in their boxes, and they're not cold with all the snow insulating the buildings.

Give them a couple of pounds of hay at night and *nothing* else or they'll get lymphangitis.'

'A couple of pounds? They'll kick their doors to bits. They're already bored being in all day.'

'Let them eat straw then. I know they'll kick up a rumpus, but it's better to have a few splintered doors than a load of sick ponies.'

He was right, as usual. I looked up lymphangitis in a horse book later and learned that enforced idleness can cause swollen legs (commonly called Monday morning leg) unless the feed ration is reduced.

No more snow fell – Sarah said there was no more left in the world as Devon had had it all – but we could see from the TV newsreels that there would be little chance of getting a council snowplough in our quiet backwater. They were all working round the clock to clear motorways, major roads and milk routes.

It was worrying for George and Valerie, as they were supposed to be flying back to Algeria in a few days' time and had things to attend to in London before they went. However, there was nothing we could do about it (Sarah's 'wishing' didn't seem to work in reverse) except tend our besieged stock as best we could and thank our lucky stars that we had plenty of animal and human feed in store.

Chapter Three

Kodak must have done well out of the Big Snow of February 1978. Everyone with a camera was busily clicking away, thinking they'd never see anything like it again. Little did we all know that this snow was but a rehearsal for the Really Big Snow of 1978–9 some ten months later.

After about five days, the minor road outside our gate became passable. Neighbouring dairy farmers, aghast at having to pour hundreds of gallons of milk away, took to their fore-end loaders and pushed a path through the middle of the road just wide enough for the milk-tanker to get through. Directly the road was clear, Brian and George dug George's car out, dried the plugs and sledged it along the drive. Once on the packed road surface, the wheels spun a bit, but George said it would be OK once it was laden with people and luggage. He and Valerie were very anxious to get away because his employers were rather heavy on people who took extra leave, whatever the excuse.

'I never did get my ride, did I?' said Sarah ruefully as they all piled in. 'I'd better not wish so hard next time.'

We waved until the car was out of sight, sorry to see them go. There are not many people you can be holed up with for a week and still be friends at the end.

A few days later the rain started, and it didn't stop until 3 March, by which time Brian and I were showing definite signs of weather paranoia. It seemed to us that ever since we left London to move to Devon the weather had gone mad. It was always being the hottest this or the wettest that and we were fed up with it. Obviously, it must have done this sort of thing before, but when you work in a town, it's just a minor inconvenience to be too hot or too cold – it doesn't actually stop you earning your living.

'Let's invite ourselves to supper with someone nice,' Brian said on one of his more despairing days, when it looked as though the earth would never be dry enough to dig again.

'Good idea. How about Liz and Graham? We haven't seen them for ages and I want to see how Liz's rabbits are coming along.'

Liz and Graham had a very small smallholding in Somerset on which they managed to squeeze a vegetable garden, a section for poultry, two breeding sows, a cow and a rabbit unit. They also had some his/her children from previous marriages, but no common ones as yet. In time, they hoped to build up their rabbitry into a profitable business, but at present Graham went out to work and Liz saw to the smallholding.

I was particularly interested in the rabbits, partly because it's always interesting to see other people's projects and partly because Liz was going to show me an ingenious new way of identifying them. (New Zealand Whites are virtually impossible to tell apart when they are housed in groups, and it's essential to know who's who when you are breeding.)

After admiring the pigs and commiserating over the water-logged garden, we went to the rabbit shed where about twenty adults and babies were housed. Liz claimed she could identify any one of them in seconds.

'Impossible,' we said.

'No, it's not. It's easy with my method,' Liz said. 'You see that one?' She pointed to a large doe who was sharing a cabbage stalk with a slightly smaller one.

'The one with blood on her ear?'

'It's not blood,' Liz said. 'It's nail varnish. Two blobs right ear. All I have to do is look at my card index and see who has right-ear markings and how many. I don't even have to pick them up, so it saves stress if they're heavily pregnant.' She flicked through some cards. 'Two blobs right. That's Africa. The one next to her is – let me see, one blob left outer – that's Bombay, India's granddaughter. She's two weeks pregnant by Parker.' She snapped the card index shut. 'Good, isn't it? Foolproof.'

'Foolproof?' said Brian. 'I'm mystified.'

'I think I've got the rough idea,' I said. 'You call them all after countries and cross-index them with ear marks. Right?'

'Parker,' interrupted Brian, 'isn't a country.' He looked at Graham for support, but Graham merely nodded and said, 'That's right. You've got the idea. Parker is completely unrelated – that's why he's been used on the India strain.'

'All the first-generation does are countries,' Liz explained. 'Africa, India, America and so on. Their daughters are called after rivers in the same countries – like Congo out of Africa – and *their* daughters are towns or mountains. It means I can keep the breeding lines pure because every name is connected to the original country.'

'And if you think our system is complicated, Brian,' said Graham, you should have seen the mess a friend of ours got into when she tried using the royal family. There aren't enough female royals to go round, so she filled the gaps with female singers. She said by the time the Duke of Kent and Shirley Bassey had had two litters, the system was so complicated that it was worse than *The Times* crossword. So she scrapped it and went back to colour coding.'

I needed a new buck. Our own buck, Hamish, had several marriageable daughters now, whom I wanted to keep. Liz said I could buy one called Volga from her. 'He's Parker's son out of Russia,' she said. 'The kids call him Zebedee. He's very sweet-natured. You could use him on Hamish's daughters and buy fresh does for Hamish.'

'*Fresh does?*' Brian slumped on to a hutch. 'I've been conned again. I thought we were coming to supper with you, not buying more rabbits. We've got a hundred already.'

'Twenty-three,' I said, 'including litters. One buck and six does on the permanent list. And you haven't been conned; I told you a month ago that Liz was going to save some rabbits for me.'

'You did,' Brian agreed gloomily. 'I thought you meant rabbits to eat.'

'We haven't been ferreting for weeks now,' Graham said.

'Not wet enough, I suppose?' Brian said icily, and we all laughed, remembering the time the four of us had spent a

November evening ferreting with an untrained spaniel in teeming rain. All we had caught was pneumonia.

We went indoors and had a lovely meal and a good chinwag, swapping snow stories and making plans for the coming season. Before we left, Liz boxed up four does for me and the buck – Volga/Zebedee – together with their record cards and instructions for applying the nail varnish to their ears.

The next morning my mother said she would help me to earmark the rabbits.

'It seems awfully complicated,' I said, looking through Liz's instructions. Anne took the folder from me and glanced at the first paragraph. 'I'm going to put Liverpool down for a draw next Saturday,' she said.

'Can we concentrate on *this* job for the moment, please?' I said snappily.

'It doesn't need much concentration to work out a four from sixteen perm,' said Anne. (Football pools are one of her many interests.) 'You've got four does. Each doe has two ears. Each ear has an inside and an outside, giving you sixteen altogether. I don't know what they taught you at that school.'

'Oh, I see what you're getting at. You mean there are sixteen choices of areas to put the nail varnish.'

'That's right. You could earmark dozens without repeating the pattern. I do think Liz is clever. How are they, by the way? Have they still got Florence and Mavis?'

'Doris and Gladys. We didn't see any of their ferrets; we stayed indoors most of the time.'

'I read an article about ferrets, or was it weasels? They have to find a mate before they're two years old or they die. Talking of which [which we weren't, but she has an amazing facility for verbal leap-frogging] I see Peter Shilton's been screwing waitresses in the back of his Mini.'

'His Mini?' I nearly dropped a rabbit. 'But he's over 6 foot tall, isn't he?'

'Mm. That's why I'm putting Liverpool down for a draw. It's bound to affect his game.'

'Hey, just a minute. Since when have you been putting bugs in Minis? How do you know he's been screwing waitresses?'

'Perhaps it was only one waitress. It was in the paper around the haddock, one of the Sundays I think. Your stars were good, by the way. You're going to have a surprise visitor and a financial gain.'

I'm still waiting for the financial gain, but the surprise visitor did appear. What with the snow and one thing and another, we had almost forgotten that we had lodged a planning application for a riding licence. Then, one day, the Town Hall sent a human instead of a form. Three humans actually, the main one and two handmaidens to carry his tape measure. Such excitement! We gave them tea and chocolate biscuits and managed not to laugh when the main man said 'egress' instead of 'way out'.

The word buzzed round the Town Hall that the tea was hot and strong at that new riding place, and soon we had sightings of Health, Planning and Veterinary. Some made appointments, some just appeared, lurked around drains and disappeared again. Fire was quite different; a friendly, helpful man, who arrived on time and without acolytes, advised us in plain English about fire hoses and where to buy them, then departed before the kettle had boiled. Later we learned that he was a real fireman, accustomed to doing brave things in burning buildings, not the sort to waste twenty minutes measuring a person's egress.

The result of all this activity was a sort of decree nisi; it's called outline planning permission and means you're nearly home and dry.

'It'll be nice to have some good news to tell at last,' I said. 'It's been nothing but bad weather stories lately.' Once a week we met our smallholding friends at evening classes and caught up on each other's news in the pub afterwards.

The Smallholders' Association, which we had helped to found the previous year, was now some 250-strong and still recruiting. Thirty or forty of us attended a thirteen-week course on animal husbandry, which had been laid on for us by the Extramural Department of Bristol University in conjunction with the Agricultural Training Board. The tutors were so good that we all risked life and limb on icy roads in order to get to the classes on time. (On one occasion, there was a power failure in Taunton, which blacked out the Evening Institute. Rather than miss our precious lesson, we all turned up with candles in jamjars and made our notes by candlelight.) It was a pleasure and a privilege to be taught by people who left you on the edge of your seat wanting more at the end of a two-hour lecture. And sometimes we got more than the two hours; for unless he made a quick getaway after class, the lecturer would be dragged off to the pub to carry on in there.

The teachers seemed to be as keen on us as we were on them. We found this rather flattering until we heard about some of the morons they had in their classes at Agricultural College. One lad was said to have sat through a series of lectures on hygiene, then solemnly recorded in his notebook: If it smells, wash it.

By the time the academic course finished, our class had learned a lot about pigs, sheep, cows, calves, hygiene, veterinary first aid and poultry. Later in the year, each subject would be followed up by a one-to-three-day practical course at an agricultural college and nearby veterinary practice: a lot to look forward to.

Meanwhile, as the days lengthened and the ground grew less wet, Brian and I concentrated on our own projects. A quite horrifying amount of money seemed to have disappeared into the smallholding and the stock, and as yet we hadn't earned a penny. Not counting petrol, our day-to-day personal expenditure was very little; we fed ourselves on home-produced meat, eggs, milk and vegetables, and the dogs on the surplus male rabbits, so all we had to buy in were things such as tea and Winalot and loo rolls. But if we wanted this happy state to continue, it was time to prime the pump.

'Another cow first, I think,' Brian said. We were sitting at the kitchen table doing what the bank manager calls forward planning. 'I'll dry Elizabeth off at the end of April, so we want one that's in milk and due to calve in the autumn.' I wrote that down and he went on: 'Sheep next. Put down "small pregnant flock".'

'That doesn't sound right,' I objected. 'We don't want midgets.'

'You can re-word it when you write the advert. What else?'

'Orphan lambs. How many shall we get?'

'How much milk are your piglets taking?'

'Three gallons.'

'Put down two lambs for the moment. Once the older piglets are sold, we'll have spare milk. If the new cow is a good milker, there might be enough for four lambs and the youngest piglets. Read it back to me.'

"Wanted: Autumn-calving Jersey house cow. Also in-lamb ewes, any breed. Also two orphan lambs."

'Put castrated,' said Brian. 'I hate doing it.'

'Oh, honestly; you are learning to be a *farmer*, aren't you?'

'I'll be a non-castrating farmer. Read the rest.'

I continued: '"For sale: 10-week-old Large White/Welsh weaners, £24 each. 7-week-old pedigree Gloucester Old Spot weaners from £30 each. All milk-fed and outdoor-reared." Is that all right?'

'I'm not sure about "from" £30 each. Are some better than others?'

'Yes – Richard. He's bigger than the rest and you can tell he's going to be really classy. I think we should run him on for a while and ask fifty for him.'

'In that case, you don't need to say "from £30". Just tell people Richard's not for sale yet.'

I phoned Betty, fellow committee member and the SHA's clearing house. She kept a list of members' wants and 'for sale' items next to her phone and saw to it that the same list was displayed at all our meetings and on the back page of the monthly newsletter.

'I've got lambs coming out of my ears,' Betty said, when I had finished dictating our list.

'I thought you might have. Got any strong ones?'

'Come and see for yourself. I've got three that might interest you.'

I took just £15 out of the teapot so that I wouldn't be tempted to buy more than three and drove over to Betty's.

'They're in here,' said Betty, opening a stable door. A sea of woolly toys surged across the straw and my heart dissolved.

I knelt in the middle of them and they sucked my fingers and bleated crossly when no milk came out.

Betty's neighbouring sheep farmers were having a dreadful spring, she told me. Those ewes that survived the recent snow were so debilitated that the effort of giving birth was killing dozens of them. Their owners, now lambing round the clock, couldn't spare the time to nurse the orphans, and were only too glad to let Betty take them home to her lamb bank. Betty was a marvel with orphans, instilling in them first the will to live, then the strength to suck. She reared them to two or three weeks old, then sold them for a few pounds each, enough to cover the costs of their milk and medication. Her expertise and hours of work she gave for nothing.

'Watch where you're kneeling,' she said. 'Two of them only came in this morning and they're scouring like mad.'

I stood up and wiped some putrid-smelling diarrhoea off my jeans. 'Which ones are ready to go, Betty?'

Betty picked up two. 'Cleo and Johnny,' she said. 'Twins. Their mother died when they were three days old, so presumably they had some colostrum at birth. They've done well; they're about a fortnight old. Now this one,' she pointed out another, 'is your best bet. I bought him in Taunton market last Saturday and he's doubled his weight in a week. I don't know where he came from or how old he is – probably four weeks – but he's a good doer, quite a character too. He *butts*. At his age, cheeky little devil.'

'I'll take the three,' I said. So began our two-year love/hate relationship with Ramrod. On the way home I suddenly realized I had forgotten to ask about castration, so I pulled into a lay-by and up-ended the two boy lambs. Johnny had a rubber castration ring round his fast-shrivelling scrotum (the whole thing atrophies and drops off in time) but Ramrod was unmistakably all there.

'He's got balls,' said Brian accusingly. He had been lying in wait for me as I drove in.

'I know. I forgot.'

'How old is he?'

'About a month. There's still time to do him.'

'I'm not doing it at a month. It's cruel.' Brian strode off to have a sulk, leaving Anne and me to give the lambs their lunchtime bottles.

'They're very small balls,' said Anne, peering under Ramrod's tail. 'I'm sure they won't be any trouble.'

Chapter Four

You reap what you sow. Whoever invented that particular piece of fiction was no gardener. What you reap for half the year is weeds (who sows weeds?), and unless you reap them hard enough, the things you *have* sown never see the light of day.

An organic gardener by inclination, Brian began to dream about Paraquat, Round Up and Asulux. He was having a difference of opinion with his rotovator, a touchy machine liable to have seizures if it saw too many thistles at one go. When it became obvious that he, Anne and I could not hand-weed the 3 acres he wanted for the commercial crop and vegetable garden, he temporarily abandoned his principles.

Drums of chemicals appeared and Brian, dressed like a spaceman, hoisted his knapsack sprayer on his back, pulled a mask over his face (to protect his lungs, not to disguise his identity) and sailed into battle. A few days later the result was clear, an overwhelming victory: Brian – millions. Weeds – nil. Nettles, thistles, bracken, docks, chickweed; their infant corpses lay satisfyingly limp on the earth.

'I'm converted,' I said. 'Can we throw away the hoes?'

'No,' Brian laughed. 'But you can have a break. I can get on with the planting now.' Paraquat, it seemed, was a contact weed-killer. It killed only what it touched, becoming inert when it reached the earth. Sooner or later all the underground weeds would be back and the blistered-hands, aching-back cycle would start all over again.

Anne and I wandered home through the orchard, leaving Brian to stake out his rows and coax the rotovator out of its sulks. 'I must start exercising the ponies now that we're not needed for weeding,' I said. 'What are you going to do?'

'Parachute jumping, I think,' said Anne, gazing up into the

branches of the apple trees. 'Just *look* at those fat buds. When it all blossoms, it's going to be a gorgeous sight. I'd like to see it from above.'

'You could stand on the cowshed roof. I'll get you a ladder if you like.'

'That's not above. I want to go in a plane.'

'Oh, a plane,' I said, uninterestedly. 'Why don't you hitch-hike to the moon while you're at it? You could see the whole globe from there.'

'Because they don't take ordinary people to the moon yet,' said Anne patiently. 'But they *do* give parachuting lessons. Quite near here as a matter of fact. I've sent away for details.'

'They wouldn't take people of your age.' I said. 'You're bound to have brittle bones by now.'

Anne played her trump. 'Didn't you see the local paper last week? A man of eighty making his first jump? It was his life's ambition, and as soon as I saw it, I thought to myself, *I'd* like to do that. So I wrote to the parachute club. I sent them a stamped addressed envelope.'

Oh, God, I thought, that means she's serious. But it won't last. Once last week's paper becomes this week's firelighter, she'll find something else.

'I've sent off for some pamphlets too,' I said, trying to change the subject. 'I want to see if I can build a wormery. I read an article about making money from worms.' I didn't say I had made enquiries about a maggotry too. Maggots are not everybody's cup of tea.

'Worms? What fun,' said Anne enthusiastically. 'How do you breed them?'

'I don't know. I'm hoping the pamphlet will explain. I've reserved Darwin on worms at the library too.'

'You'll be able to write funny adverts for them – "Earn from Worms" and so on. I wonder what they eat.'

'I think they eat leaves and rubbish. Wouldn't it be convenient if they ate dung? I could rear them on the ponies' muck heap.'

'When are you going to get some customers for those idle ponies? They're getting fat.'

'Clients,' I said. Riding customers are called clients, according to my manual. It sounds better.'

'Sounds like plain snobbery to me. You're not selling a professional service, you're selling an hour of a pony's time.'

Brian and I had given some thought to the question of what to call the riding business. Not a school, or the customers/clients might think they were going to learn something; not a trekking centre or I would get holidaymakers in plimsolls turning up for day-long rides, and not a centre. Centre is actually quite a good word for DIY or gardening establishments, but it sounded a bit too all-embracing for the sort of light hacking I was going to offer. In the end we settled for 'Riding Stables' which looked feeble on paper but surprisingly good on a white board painted by a professional sign-writer.

I studied my instruction manual over and over. I didn't much like its 'toadying to the client' attitude, nor its apparent disregard for horses' comforts, but as its contributors plainly knew more about the business than I did – not difficult – I decided to abide by it. I also decided to take the ponies and myself in hand; we were all unfit ('roughed off for the winter' is the correct expression, and one that I found wholly appropriate when I looked in the mirror), so I set aside three hours a day to tone us all up.

It was great fun exploring the lanes and bridlepaths. The woods on the nearby Blackdown Hills were owned by the Forestry Commission, and they had obligingly cut wide grassy tracks between the trees (fire breaks) which made wonderful rides. I rode the ponies in pairs, leading one from another – Monty and Wellington, then Noah and Rocky. Rebel and Jinks I took separately as I didn't yet know them well enough to control two together.

One weekend our twelve-year-old, horse-mad niece, Sally, came to stay. We took Rebel and Jinks for exercise – the first time they had been out together since I had had them – and I was just saying to Sally how pleased I was with the new 'lodgers' when Rebel started to play up. He had been fine as a solo ride but now, in company with Jinks, he was nothing but trouble. The problem was that he simply couldn't bear to be parted from his stable-mate, and every time there was more than 20 or 30 yards between them, he panicked, deposited his rider on the ground, and hurried back to Jinks's side.

At first, Sally and I didn't realize that he was doing it deliberately, but after being thrown twice each, the penny dropped.

'What are we going to do?' asked Sally. 'He's *lethal*.' There are many ways of curing a horse of dangerous behaviour, but mine was the simplest. 'We're going to phone Tony,' I said.

Tony took a serious view. 'The two of them *must* be separated,' he said. 'Permanently. Tell the owners what happened and if they can't find another home for him, I'll have him for a while.'

Rebel's owners, hundreds of miles away in an army camp, readily agreed to the transfer, so Tony took him away for deconditioning. It was a long process and Rebel didn't give in without a fight. The outcome was that, far from becoming a reformed character, Rebel transferred his dependence from Jinks to Tony and would allow nobody but Tony to ride him. (One experienced horsewoman tried and Rebel broke her jaw.) So for the time being that was that. Tony kept Rebel for his sole use and we had to look around for a replacement.

It, or rather he, was not long coming. He was an exceptionally pretty skewbald, 11 hands, no hang-ups – just the job. His name was Jonathan and his owner kept him as a pet, but wanted him worked for six months to stop him getting too fat.

Fed up with waiting for the final planning permission, and fed up with not having any money, I put an advert in the local paper: 'Accompanied riding in the Blackdown Hills, quiet ponies, no road work, beginners welcome'.

'Beginners welcome?' said Brian, puzzled. 'I thought you didn't particularly want beginners.'

'Well, I could hardly say so in the advert, could I? "Dislikes beginners" wouldn't be very good for business.'

'I don't see why you had to mention beginners at all.'

'Because, fathead, all the other riding adverts say "beginners welcome". It's like the way au pairs always say "fond of children". Doesn't mean a thing.'

The local paper came out on Fridays, so I was rather surprised to get an answer to my advert on Thursday evening. It was from a Mrs Lacey wanting to book a one-hour ride on Saturday morning.

'How did you get a copy of the paper a day early?' I asked. She said she didn't know it was a day early; hers was always delivered on Thursday evenings. When I told Brian, he said no wonder all the best bargains had gone by Friday if half the readers had already had a twelve-hour start.

I stayed within earshot of the phone all the next day. By teatime, things were looking good. I had lots of calls; six more bookings for Saturday, one for Sunday, two horse insurance companies touting for business and one heavy breather. (He rang when I was half-way down the garden and by the time I had run back and picked up the phone I was breathing heavily too, most confusing for him.) Then, in the evening, four more people booked one-hour rides for Sunday, and several SHA members phoned wanting to buy piglets.

'It's going to be a busy weekend,' I said. Brian was reading something and didn't answer.

'I said it's going to be a busy weekend,' I repeated. He looked up, a pained expression on his face, and said, 'Have you *seen* today's post?'

'No, I haven't had time. What is it – another final demand?'

'Huh, final demand. A final demand would be poetry compared to this.' He stabbed a finger on a printed sheet: 'What the bloody hell is a *maggotry*?'

'Oh, good, it's come. There should be something about a wormery too. Is it there?'

'If by "it" you mean this – this *script* for a horror film, yes it's here. It's a good job I've had supper.'

I started to read the maggot leaflet aloud: 'Part One. The Fly House.'

'I don't want to hear any more, thank you. I've read enough – more than enough. I think I'll go and shut up the chickens.' The dogs followed him out. 'Traitors,' I muttered, and returned to 'The Fly House'.

Happy flies sound right, I learned. Well, that was OK,

wasn't it? Nothing like a horror script. I read on. The happiness of one's flies, it seemed, was the key to success in the commercial maggotry. They didn't need much to make them happy – sugar and water supplements for the expectant mothers or egg-laying flies, and meat for everyone placed on clean newspaper. (*Clean* newspaper? For flies?) The thing to do was to get them all sucking away at the blood and juice without interruption. There would be casualties, naturally, but the operator was not to worry about crunching dead flies and maggots underfoot, it was something you quickly got used to.

Colour prejudice ruled. Plain colours – yellow for English fishermen, red for Germans – meant higher profits. Mixed maggots were no good, nor were thin ones. In order to get your youngsters to grow quickly into big, fat, teenage maggots, you had to ensure a plentiful supply of fresh, raw meat. They were fussy about temperature too: 32°F kept them in suspended animation prior to shipping. If the refrigerated containers broke down – strewth! It *was* like a horror script. It seemed to me that if the refrigerated containers broke down, the maggot farmer would need either a good lawyer or a one-way ticket to Australia.

The pamphlet ended, 'It is essential to obtain planning permission before setting up commercially.' Oh, well, that was that. If it took four months to legalize six ponies, what would the Town Hall make of several million bluebottles?

Brian came in looking glazed. 'Where are the dogs?' I said.

'Anne's taken them all for a run. Did you know she's going to join a parachute club? She's jogging round the orchard – in training, she says.'

'Oh, that's just a passing fancy. Some old boy made a parachute jump last week and she's envious. It'll pass. By the way, it says here that you have to have planning permission for maggots. I haven't read "Worms" yet.'

Brian went over to the sink and filled the kettle. 'I'm living in a loony bin,' he muttered. 'My mother-in-law is going to jump out of aeroplanes and you're going to start a typhoid epidemic. What's the *matter* with everyone?'

'It's the spring,' I said. 'Everyone's coming out of hibernation. I've got twelve rides booked for the weekend, how about that?'

'Marvellous, £24. How much was the advert?'

'Under £2. It was about fifteen words at 9 pence a word. If you're making tea, can I have mine in the bath, please? I'm going to have a lovely long soak with a book and then an early night. There's a Mrs Lacey coming at nine tomorrow, so I must get all the feeds done by eight.'

Mrs Lacey was ten minutes early for her ride. Fortyish, thin, with an occult-looking pendant and an anxious expression, she said she had to get out of the house as things were getting her down. I didn't have to say 'What things?' because it was obvious I was going to get an earful whether I liked it or not.

'You're a bit strung up,' I said, forgetting she was The Client. 'Try to relax.'

'Will do,' she said. She sprang lightly on to Wellington's back, adjusted her stirrups and took deep breaths through alternating nostrils. Presumably, this was in accordance with some yin/yang teaching, but it didn't seem very effective. Her neck sinews came up like a relief map. I said hurriedly, 'Shall we go for a ride in the woods?' If she relaxed any harder, she was going to faint.

We plodded up the track and she said did I have children and I said yes. 'Why do we *bother*?' she said, the neck sinews in evidence again. 'Why, why, *why*?'

'They can be ghastly,' I sympathized, remembering the hour-long battles I used to have with Sara over shoes, food and late hours. Battles a mother has to win while the child is still growing, or she'll have a wrinkled, bunioned, accusing twenty-year-old on her hands. 'How old is your daughter, Mrs Lacey?'

'Eighteen.'

'You really mustn't worry, you know. By eighteen, you've done your whack. They all go through dodgy phases. What's she doing – sleeping around?'

'Sleeping around? Oh, God, if only she was. She's a virgin – a bloody *virgin* – after all we've done for her!'

I couldn't think of anything to say. There are no comforting clichés for mothers of virgins. I suggested she contacted the Rare Breeds Trust, but Mrs Lacey was not amused.

'She's getting married.' Through clenched teeth the distraught mother divulged her awful secret. 'To a *bank clerk*. In a *church*.' That seemed to be three awful secrets – well, four if you counted the virginity, but perhaps after the wedding ceremony that could be crossed off.

Tamsin, it seemed, had been a problem from the start. Despite a Rudolph Steiner primary education followed by Dartington, she had doggedly conformed (even got a crush on the games mistress) and had left school at eighteen with good A-levels and a bent for needlework. She then enrolled on a cookery course, got engaged to a trainee bank clerk and broke her mother's heart.

'Married,' Mrs Lacey repeated. 'I can't face my friends at the moment, I really can't.' Her friends had pot-smoking children, laid-back vegans, in and out of each other's bed like rabbits.

'What does your husband think?'

'He thinks it's funny. He reads Spinoza.'

What I know about Spinoza could be written on half a greenshield stamp, but I didn't want her to think I was thick, so I nodded wisely and pulled the conversation down to a less demanding level. 'Where are they going to live, Tamsin and er – ?'

'Mark. He's called Mark.'

'Really? I've got a Marc. Marcus actually, but he likes Marc with a c. Says it's more charismatic.'

'Mark the clerk hasn't got hormones, never mind charisma. His parents are going to lend them the deposit for a *bungalow*.' She bit her lip. 'At the rate things are going, they'll have kids called Cheryl and Beryl and a crinoline lady over the loo roll. He already gives her those awful heart-shaped birthday cards – you know, "To the Best Girl in the World" written on a lump of red eiderdown.'

The ride certainly didn't seem to be helping her to forget her troubles, but when we got back, she said she had enjoyed it and booked again for the following week.

'What do you know about Spinoza?' I asked Brian later.

'Actor, I think. Oh, no, that's Spinetti. Spinoza philosophized, didn't he?' That was the total of our pooled knowledge about Spinoza, despite being avid listeners to *Round Britain Quiz*. Ashamed, we looked him up. It seemed he believed that things are never as bad as you think they're going to be. But then, as Brian pointed out, Mrs Spinoza had probably never sent off a pre-paid envelope for details about breeding maggots.

Chapter Five

The piglets fetched good prices, particularly the Gloucester Old Spots, which all went to breeding homes. This hardy old breed was in demand again. Like everything else, pig fashions come and go, and now, with feed prices rocketing, the small pig-keeper, unable to cut costs by bulk buying, was rediscovering the advantages of Spots.

Rosie and Phyll were crossbred sows, excellent in their way, but obviously not capable of producing the more valuable pedigree offspring we wanted. Their piglets nearly always went to smallholders who wanted a couple of pigs to fatten. For some time we had been thinking of selling them and buying two GOS to replace them, but until now the right home had not come along.

Then, one day, a young woman phoned up, introduced herself as Zoe and said that she and her husband had heard we had some piglets for sale. 'We're complete beginners,' she said, and I laughed and told her about putting 'beginners welcome' in my riding advert. 'Tell me about yourselves,' I said. 'We're very particular about where our pigs go.'

'Yes, I heard you were. Is it true you won't sell single piglets?'

'That's right. Pigs get dreadfully lonely on their own. We sell breeding boars singly because the people who buy them already have sows, but otherwise they're all sold in pairs. What did you have in mind, a couple of weaners for the freezer?'

'No, two females for breeding. We'd prefer adult sows really so that we wouldn't have to wait too long for litters, but I don't suppose you sell sows?'

'Well, we don't normally, but we were thinking of selling two crossbred sows because we want to stick to Gloucester Old Spots in future. Have you got plenty of ground for pigs?

And fencing?' I went on to more personal questions like how much did her husband earn and did they get on well together. (I didn't want Phyll and Rosie starving on the dole or becoming pigs of a broken marriage.)

Zoe was very good-natured about these enquiries, as in fact all animal lovers are, and told me of their smallholding plans. They lived with her husband's grandmother in a large house with dry outbuildings and 8 acres of grass. 'Drained?' I asked anxiously, and was assured that Howard, the husband, was seeing to this.

'It sounds perfect,' I said, 'and I'm sure Rosie and Phyll would suit you. They're very quiet and friendly, both pregnant too. Would you like us to deliver them?'

'Yes, please, if it's not too much trouble. I'll order straw and pig nuts and have everything ready before you come.' She gave me the address and directions for finding it, and we settled on a delivery date for a few days hence.

'They live in Dorset,' I told Brian later. He loves maps and was pleased to have an excuse to pore over his Ordnance Survey maps of Dorset, a county that neither of us knew well. He soon found Zoe's house. 'Whew,' he said. 'They must be fairly well off – it's a pricey area.'

'Howard's grandmother owns the house,' I said. 'His parents were killed in a car accident – isn't that *awful*? He's only twenty-one. He did architecture at college, and he works in –'

'All right, all right,' Brian laughed. 'Do you realize you take more trouble over who the pigs live with than who Marcus and Sara live with?'

'Of course I do. The animals are totally dependent on us. If Sara was ill-treated by Gerry, she could just leave him. Pigs can't get on a train.'

Nor, it would appear, could they get into a Transit van. When the day came to load Phyll and Rosie we had a terrible time with them. Their feet were killing them, they said, sitting down firmly – can't go another step; what – us go up that nasty steep ramp? You must be joking.

We coaxed and threatened and even sacrificed a whole packet of chocolate biscuits, but they wouldn't budge.

Eventually, Brian was forced to do a rather expensive Sir Walter Raleigh act: he nailed a brand new piece of haircord carpet to an old oak door and used that as a ramp instead of the wobbly planks. Phyll and Rosie tested it for safety, then condescended to walk slowly in. We could have killed them.

Brian drove and I navigated. Well, strictly speaking, he drove and I held the map. I think map-makers have a vested interest in divorce – why else do they always put roads in where there aren't any?

'There it is.' I pointed triumphantly, some two hours later. Brian sighed and reversed the van. We were glad to get there. The 'why-didn't-you-tell-me-before-we-had-to-turn' countered by 'you-drive-too-fast-for-me-to-see-anything' dialogue was over for the time being.

It was an imposing old house on three floors, quite unusual for an isolated country area, and in the inevitable state of shabbiness we had come to associate with smallholdings. (Drainage and creosote and fencing soon swallow up any spare cash.) We parked the van and went up some stone steps to the front door, which was propped open with a *Reader's Digest* DIY manual. Inside the hall there were two more front doors – one of stripped oak, the other gleaming with fresh white paint and brass fittings. We knocked at the raw wooden one and waited.

'They're probably outside,' I said after a few minutes. 'Shall we go and look?'

'Just a sec. I'll try the other door first.' He knocked.

'Who is it?' An old voice, Howard's grandmother presumably.

'Brian and Faith,' said Brian, 'and pigs.'

'Oh, yes, pigs. I'll put my teeth in. Just a moment.' For some reason Brian thought this was creasingly funny. There was a shuffling and tapping, then the door was opened by a neat little figure in a dusky pink cashmere dress. The fragile granny image was somewhat marred by the meat cleaver she was holding in her right hand and which she now transferred to her left.

'Constance Straker,' she said, shaking hands with Brian.

Yes, I thought, you would need your teeth in to say Constance Straker. Perhaps mothers should think of things like that before they choose names for newborn babies. Goodness knows, they're giving you enough clues with their gummy little faces. Would *Marcus* have to have dentures one day? Impossible. All that cod-liver oil...

'My wife, Faith,' Brian said, with a glare that meant he had already said it at least once. I came back to earth.

'How do you do, Mrs Straker,' I said. 'I'm sorry if we startled you. We're looking for Zoe and Howard actually, but there's no reply at the other door.'

'You didn't startle me.' She saw us looking at the meat cleaver and laughed. 'I was chopping up the dogs' marrow bones – they're too big to go in the saucepan.'

'You shouldn't be doing that,' said Sir Galahad Brian. 'Let me do it.'

'*Would* you? How kind. The kitchen is through here.' I followed them in, wondering how soon I could acquire white hair and a pink cashmere dress if that was the way to get marrow bones split.

Mrs Straker's kitchen and sitting-room were divided by a counter with a tiled top. 'Howard made it,' she said. 'He's a dear boy, very *flexible* in his work. This was supposed to be a wall with a serving hatch, but he kept altering it as he went along. I quite like it now; it's handy having a surface for hot dishes.'

Brian chopped the bones on the kitchen step, then Mrs Straker directed us to the part of the grounds where she thought we would find Zoe and Howard. Before we had gone far, Zoe came running across a lawn and apologized for not meeting us when we arrived. 'We've hired a petrol-driven cement mixer,' she said. 'It makes such a racket you can't hear cars coming up the drive. I'll show you the pigs' place first, then you must meet Howard.' She led us to some rather grandiose farm buildings opening out on to a large paddock.

'Is it Victorian?' asked Brian, fingering the ornate wrought-iron railings round the top of the pigsty.

'It's probably a mixture of periods; most of these old places are. This part would have been built as dog kennelling originally – it's ideal for pigs, though, isn't it?'

'It's lovely,' I said. 'They must have thought a lot of their dogs in those days. Imagine what this must have cost – tiled floor, central drainage channel, piped water, the lot.'

'And it's draughtproof,' said Zoe. 'It's much warmer here than in the servants' old bedrooms, but of course servants were cheaper than dogs then. Howard's going to put central heating in if we can get a grant. He's very clever,' she added, 'he's building a sunken garden. We're going to plant heliotrope and formal box hedges and – oh, I *am* sorry. Shouldn't we be unloading the pigs?'

'No, that's all right,' said Brian. 'They'll be fine in the van for a while; they can sleep off the journey. I'd like to see your sunken garden first.'

Zoe took us across a thistly field and stopped when the ground fell away steeply. 'There,' she said proudly.

'Good God,' said Brian and lit a cigarette.

It was not so much a sunken garden as an open-cast mine. There were mounds of shale and gravel and boulders tipped haphazardly in a depression the size of a tennis court. Brackish water swirled two inches deep over the entire surface. Howard was cementing something in the middle and waved his trowel when he saw us. 'Hi,' he called cheerfully. 'What do you think of it?'

I glanced apprehensively at Brian and hoped he wasn't going to say what he really thought of it, but I needn't have worried. Like Howard, he too can see potential in unlikely places, the Taj Mahal in a Dorset cesspit.

'Got yourself quite a project here, haven't you, Howard?' he said. Howard scrambled out of the pit and several lumps of stone which had been balanced precariously on other lumps of stone toppled into the water. 'Damn,' he said. 'I can't make the cement stick. I think I must have made it too runny.'

'How deep are you making the foundations for your walls?' Brian asked.

'They're not walls; they're going to be Roman arches. I'm not doing foundations – I thought the weight of the stones would stabilize the bases.'

'But they've already fallen over,' Brian pointed out gently. 'Perhaps if you lowered the water table?...'

'It would make a nice pond,' I contributed, meaning the whole thing would look better flooded.

'I'm going to make a little pool at the end,' said Howard, 'with a fountain. What's a water table, Brian?'

Brian said curiously: 'Where did you study architecture?'

'London. I only did one term. God, it was boring – just a lot of old history. It gave me some super ideas, though.'

'Don't you think it might be a good idea to get a builder to, um, start you off here?' said Brian.

'A builder? We don't want builders, do we, Zoe? They've no *vision*.'

'They don't need vision,' Brian said patiently. 'They know how to make things stay up.'

Howard agreed that Brian had a point there. 'Maybe I'll scrap the Roman arches,' he said. 'Well, not scrap them, turn them into columns. Would you like Doric columns, Zo? They wouldn't take so much cement. (I saw now why his grandmother had ended up with a counter top instead of a whole kitchen wall.) Zoe said Doric columns would be lovely 'with wisteria trailing round in spirals'.

'Hydrangea,' said Brian. 'It does well in wet places.' He looked at his watch: 'Shall we get the pigs unloaded now? Your grandmother has invited us in for sherry before we leave – we'd better not keep her waiting.'

'Sherry?' said Zoe. 'That's a good sign. She hasn't been very well lately. Her new dentures make her mouth sore.'

'She's very nice, isn't she?' I said. 'Active for her age too. She was wielding a chopper when we arrived.'

'She'll hack her finger off one of these days,' Zoe said. But she hardly ever lets us help her. She says she doesn't feel eighty-three, so why should she act it.'

Rosie and Phyll thoroughly approved of their new kennel-cum-sty, and after rooting through the straw to see if anyone just happened to have dropped a packet of biscuits, they walked out to sample their field. This evidently merited a five-star rating too, and before long they were ploughing their noses along the turf and grunting with pleasure at each tasty morsel they turned up.

'They're fabulous. So clean and so *friendly*.' Howard wasn't going to get many Doric columns built today, it seemed. He and Zoe patted the pigs and scratched them behind the ears. We showed them how to make a pig roll on to its back like a dog, and how to check them for minor ailments. 'I've written all this down for you,' I said. 'But if there's anything you're not sure about, like ringing or worming, just phone us.'

'Ringing? What's ringing?'

'Putting rings through their noses,' Brian explained. 'If you want them to graze a pasture rather than dig it up, you have to ring them. At the moment it would be better to leave them unringed so that they can root out all these thistles in the field, but later on in the year you can ring them to protect the grass roots. The point is, don't try to do it yourselves.'

'Why, is it difficult?'

'It's not difficult, but it hurts them. What we do in the Smallholders' Association is to ring each others' pigs so that no pig is hurt by its own people. They're so trusting, you see. It would be like operating on your own child.'

I knelt down and put an arm round each pig. 'Bye, Rosie. Bye, Phyll. You've got a lovely home here, so be good girls.' I gave them some Polos and stood up. Brian pulled their ears and told them to have lots of big litters for Zoe and Howard, then we all went indoors and had sherry with Howard's gran.

A few days later I found myself thinking of Mrs Straker's meat cleaver again and wishing I had one to silence the human battleship in our stable-yard. Her name was Mrs Prentice, and the only career she could have been apprenticed to would have been heavyweight boxing. Her daughter, Lalage, was a *ninny*, she informed me in a voice that sounded as though she smoked forty cigars a day. Lalage's shortcomings were then listed, with much finger stabbing in my arm to emphasize each point.

'Ski? Broke her damned *leg* on the second day.' Poke, poke. 'Can't swim – turns blue.' More poke. 'Tried ballet; waste of time, the dancing mistress said. Tennis, piano, skating – hopeless. No co-ordination.' This formidable woman was much taller than me and I had to keep my wits about me to avoid the finger going straight in my eye.

'So you want me to try to teach Lalage to ride then?' I said, looking at Lalage with what I hoped was an encouraging smile. She did look a lost cause – very tall and stringy, almost boneless, like a tapeworm.

'Try is the word,' said Mrs Prentice. 'I don't expect you to have any more success than the other riding schools. I'm a fair woman' – the mighty forefinger caught me unawares on the shoulder – 'and I won't blame you when you fail. She's a complete ninny.' We seemed to be starting the reel again, so I said hurriedly, 'Which riding school has Lalage been going to?' and clutched the wall for support when she told me. 'But Mrs Prentice, that's the best riding school in the West Country – some of the Olympic horses have trained there. I couldn't possibly...'

'You're cheaper,' said Mrs Prentice firmly. 'I've been paying £6 an hour there, and all she does is fall off. She may as well fall off for £2 an hour.' It sounded a crazy way of spending the housekeeping, but it takes all sorts. 'How old are you, Lalage?' I asked. 'Thirteen,' said Lalage.

Oh, four-letter word. I am not that keen on teenage girls anyway, but ask any teacher which age group they most dread and the answer is always the same – thirteen. At thirteen the human female is at its very worst: the hormones are in an uproar, it doesn't know if it is animal, vegetable or mineral, and identity crisis coincides with an unparalleled spurt of physical growth. Girls of thirteen fall over their feet, get their sums wrong, hate their parents and fall in love with sixth-formers (boys if you're lucky). We have all been thirteen; the miracle is that so many of us made it to fourteen.

'That's nice,' I said lamely, 'and you do like riding?'

'I don't mind.'

'See what I mean?' said Mrs Prentice. 'A ninny.'

'I'll get my appointments book,' I said, and dived into my beloved tack room, my haven of good smells. Mrs Prentice followed me in and sniffed approvingly. 'Nice tack,' she said, 'but it's rather dark in here, isn't it? Why don't you have a light on?'

'Oh, er, we haven't had electricity laid on yet. I use an oil lamp sometimes, but I'm used to it like this now.' The real reason I liked it dark was that I didn't want anyone to see how empty my appointments book was. Empty of appointments, that is. I don't like blank pages, so I had filled every page from January to March with stories. To anyone glancing at it in the dark it looked as though business was booming.

'I can fit her in at ten o'clock tomorrow morning,' I said, putting my hand over the end of a children's story about a dog who thinks the world has come to an end because he gets a cold and can't smell anything. 'There's an eight-year-old coming at ten o'clock but she's off the leading rein, so I'll be able to take care of Lalage and see she doesn't fall off, ha ha.'

Mrs Prentice bristled. She didn't want to hear about capable eight-year-olds. 'Ten a.m. then,' she said. 'I'll be here.'

That's what I was afraid of. My instructors' manual stated that young clients would make better progress if not distracted. In other words – get rid of the mothers. But it didn't say how.

Eight-year-old Fiona and her mother arrived at 9.45 the next morning. They were from Edinburgh, the mother explained, spending a few days in Taunton, where her husband was on a business trip. 'I hope you don't mind us getting here early,' she said, 'but Fiona couldn't wait. She had to miss her Saturday ride at home last week because of this trip.'

'I don't mind at all,' I said. 'She can help me to get the ponies ready.'

'May I groom one, please? I love ponies.' Fiona's accent was irresistible, the rolled r in 'groom' and 'poonies' for ponies. Lovely.

'Sorry,' I said, 'I've already groomed them. But you can put some saddles and bridles on. Come on, I'll introduce you to Jonathan – he's the pony you'll be riding.'

'I'll be off now,' said her mother. 'See you at eleven, Fiona. Have a nice ride.'

'Bye, Mummy. Er…a wee bit after eleven…?'

'Eleven. Mrs Addis won't want you getting in the way.'

'Do leave her if you'd like to,' I said. 'I haven't got anyone else after eleven, so she can do some grooming when we get back.'

How easy it is, sometimes, to create small heavens. Fiona skipped across the yard looking like a dog that's been promised a walk. Her mother thanked me quietly and drove away.

Fiona and I had Jonathan, Noah and Wellington all ready by the time Mrs Prentice's open-topped car drove in. 'Blow the cobwebs away,' she boomed, indicating the car. 'Come on Lalage, chop chop, don't keep people waiting.' Lalage slid out of the car. She looked better in jodhpurs and hacking jacket, but the tall, lanky frame topped by a hard hat still slouched. Mrs Prentice straightened Lalage's shoulders as if she was kneading dough. 'Hold your head up,' she commanded, 'remember the rider's code: "Your head and your heart keep *up*, your hands and your heels keep *down*..."'

'...Your knees keep close to your horse's sides and your elbows close to your own,' Fiona finished with a grin.

'Hello, Lalage,' I said, feeling brave with Fiona to support me. 'Come and meet everyone. This is Fiona' – the girls nodded to each other – 'and this is your pony, Wellington. I'll just tighten his girths and you can mount. Do you want a leg up?'

'I don't mind,' said Lalage. Conscious of Mrs Prentice's eyes boring into the back of my head, I heaved Lalage into the saddle and adjusted the stirrups. Fiona checked Jonathan's girths and sprang aboard. 'Pretty, pretty Jonathan,' she crooned and patted his neck. 'We're going for a ride in the woods. Isn't that lovely?'

Mrs Prentice, who had been quiet for all of five minutes, turned to me and barked: 'In the *woods*? On a *hack*? My dear girl, Lalage needs *lunging*!'

And you need strangling, you old cow, I thought. I smiled innocently and said: 'Fiona's mother insisted on a hack for Fiona, Mrs Prentice. She's never been to Devon before and she's *so* looking forward to seeing some of the countryside.' I winked at Fiona, who didn't show any surprise at this thumping lie, mounted Noah and took Wellington's leading rein. 'See you at eleven – bye.' We clattered out of the yard.

I had actually intended to go on foot, leading Lalage, but

had changed my mind when it struck me that Mrs Prentice might try to come too if she saw me walking. Mounted, we were able to make a quick getaway. We rode briskly along the grass verges and when I was sure the coast was clear I turned off into the woods. 'Right, girls, slow down now,' I said. 'We'll take it easy up the hill. You OK, Lalage?'

'Yes, thank you,' said Lalage. 'I like Wellington.' It was not what my book would call Pupil Progress, but it was a start.

'Why are you on the leading rein, Lalage?' asked Fiona.

'I've had some accidents,' said Lalage.

'Nasty things, accidents.' Fiona sounded more like eighty than eight. 'My brother caught his penis in his zip when he was younger. Puir little Bruce, he had to go to hospital.'

'Penis?' said Lalage, suddenly coming to life. 'You mean…his …thingy?' She put her hand to her mouth and giggled.

'His *penis*,' said Fiona scornfully. 'You know – all boys have them. It was a near thing the doctor said. They had to circumcize him.'

'I've heard of circumcize,' said Lalage with relish. 'Jewish boys have their thingies cut off when they're teenagers, then they have a party afterwards. A barbecue, or something.'

'No, Lalage,' I began, but shut up when I saw how enthralled she was. Besides, I wanted to hear more about these poor barbecued boys.

'Bruce didn't have a party,' said Fiona. 'Perhaps they don't in Scotland. He didn't have it all cut off either, just sort of tidied up.'

'Have you *seen* it, then?' Lalage was impressed. Reluctantly I decided it was time to intervene. 'Now, girls, that's enough chatter,' I said. 'This is supposed to be a ride, not a hen party. Fiona, shorten your reins and prepare to trot, please.'

After an hour, Lalage's riding had not improved at all but I hoped the experience might increase her status at school a notch or two. After all, not many girls could say that they had met a girl whose brother had had his thingy cut off.

Chapter Six

John and Lin, the couple who had bought our guest-house the previous year, continued to run it as a holiday home for unaccompanied children. They were much better at it than we had been, so good in fact that they only ever had one assistant (a nice lad called Kim) for the holiday children, whereas we had had four. Of course, the fact that they already had five of their own helped; noise and lost sandals and tears at bedtime didn't send them round the bend as it had done us.

Instead of buying ponies for their guests to ride, they very sensibly decided to hire ours instead. (Ponies are like old cars – cheap to buy but expensive to license and insure.) Twice a week John brought a busload of children to us and each child would have an hour or a half-hour ride, depending on numbers.

The rides started at Easter. It was quite like old times, walking round the lanes leading a string of ponies and chattering children, and bliss to know that we could hand them back afterwards for someone else to feed. Some of them, who had been our own guests the previous year, were amazed to find us in a new setting. They seemed to see themselves as a sort of liberating force, people who brought relief to poor Brian and Faith, shut away on their quiet farm with nobody to talk to.

John and his student helper, Kim, were amused at the way the children compared the new regime to the old: 'Lin's a *much* better cook than Faith...Kim plays proper football...trifle with walnuts twice this week...didn't have to go to bed till ten last night.' Pillow fights, midnight feasts, bawdy songs; we heard how our successors *encouraged* these hitherto forbidden delights. All lies, of course, as John was at pains to point out. If anything, he said, he and Lin were in favour of more discipline, holiday or no holiday. 'We've been very easy on those two, though,' he said, nodding towards two small boys who were deep in discussion about some bygone test match. 'Walsh and Sinclair. They're not quite as tough as they think they are.'

'What are their first names?' I asked. 'You don't call them Walsh and Sinclair, surely?'

'We do, actually; they insist. It's all part of the stiff-upper-lip act.'

Walsh and Sinclair were both eight and a half. They had been sent away to prep school at the age of seven, and spent the school holidays with anybody's family but their own. They were funny little scraps, like two elderly barristers to listen to; they called each other by their surnames and addressed every adult male as 'sir'. The other children called them Marks and Spencer because they did everything together, and gave them quite a lot of stick over their plummy accents. Walsh and Sinclair took all the teasing good-naturedly, even when their cries of 'pax' fell on deaf ears. The other children thought pax was a chocolate bar and just carried on tormenting them.

'And how are you two getting on?' John asked, after bringing us up to date on all the Upottery news. 'How are the pansy and pony businesses doing?'

'Anemones,' said Brian. I looked at him in surprise. This was the first I had heard about anemones. 'Sorry, I forgot to tell you,' he continued. 'I've ordered 20,000 anemone corms – about half an acre – and 15,000 mixed chrysanth plants.'

I'm not able to visualize any number greater than ten, so I took this news calmly. (If I had known what we were in for, I would definitely have caught the next train to Inverness and stayed there for the flowering season.)

'That sounds ambitious,' said John. 'Lin loves anemones, so save me a few bunches, won't you? It's her birthday soon.'

Brian laughed. 'They won't be flowering until August, I'm afraid. I shall plant in June and pick from August to the first frosts.'

Later, over lunch, Brian showed Anne and me the anemone catalogue. The Rosewarne Experimental Station in Cornwall had just completed trials of a new strain called St Piran, a very large-flowering hardy plant, as yet not available to the general public, but reserved for commercial growers only.

My mother is not innumerate. '*Twenty thousand*!' she squealed. 'Who on earth is going to pick?'

'We'll manage somehow,' said Brian. 'There's three of us, and I expect my mother would come for August.' He carefully didn't remind us that *each* anemone plant would produce not one but dozens of flowers. Anne and I are keen on gardening, too, and if the phone had not rung at that moment, we would have remembered that anemones are multiple bloomers.

'I'll get it,' I said. 'It might be a booking.'

It was. A family of four holidaying in Devon wanted a two-hour ride that same afternoon. I said that would be fine and made a note of their names and weights. After ringing off, I transferred these details into my diary, then remembered I hadn't asked if any of them could ride.

'Blast,' I said, returning to the table. 'I forgot to ask what experience they've had.'

'They?' said Brian.

'Mm, it was four. For two hours. I was so bucked at the thought of £8 all in one go that I forgot.'

'No wonder you two are always broke,' Anne said to Brian. 'Shall I buy her a calculator?'

'It's sixteen,' Brian explained carefully to me. 'Four people for two hours at £2 an hour equals £16.'

'That's another strange thing,' I said. 'She gave me their weights in pounds not stones.'

'It's the Common Market,' Anne said. 'It gets into everything. My old cooker never worked properly after it went centigrade.'

'Did she sound foreign – the mother?' Brian said. 'I can't imagine English people knowing what they weigh in pounds.'

'No, she didn't. She had quite a West Country brogue. What's 140 lb?'

'Ten stone. Didn't she mind telling you she weighed 10 stone?'

'No, 10 stone was him. She's around 120 or "waan twenny" as she put it. What are you laughing at?'

'You. That's not a West Country accent – it's American. Do some more in her voice.' He listened as I mimicked my customer, then said, 'You've booked yourself a family of Mexicans by the sound of it.'

I was very impressed. I didn't know he had a Professor Higgins ear. As it turned out, not only was he correct about the accent, he wasn't far off geographically either.

They came from a place about 2 inches short of New Mexico in our atlas, and had all 'ridden horseback' since they were embryos. (This big, said the mother, indicating the distance between her thumb and forefinger.) But 'horseback' American style is not riding as we know it, and soon I was in deep trouble.

Everything began well enough. They emptied out of their car and smiled big American smiles. 'Hi! Sarnyer and Tarm, Tarm junior and Nancy.' I interpreted this correctly as meaning 'How do you do. My name is Sonia and this is my husband Tom, son Tom and daughter Nancy.' The children ran over to the waiting ponies and stroked them while the parents 'whewed' and 'geed' at the beauty of the old thatched house. They were a thoroughly nice family, and when Sonia assured me that they had all ridden since they were 'this big', I felt sure we were all going to have a very pleasant couple of hours.

I tightened the ponies' girths and indicated which pony was for which rider. 'If you would take the black one, Tom – he's called Monty – and you, Sonia, on Jinks, please. I'll help the children while you get acquainted.' I helped Nancy, a wiry six-year-old, on to Jonathan. She beamed happily and patted his neck. 'What's her name?' she asked.

'He's a boy, actually. He's called Jonathan.'

'Oh, sorry, Jonathan. You're so pretty I thought you were a girl.'

I unhitched Noah and walked down the yard to open the gate. 'This way, everybody. We'll turn left out of the gate and head up the hill over there.' I glanced over my shoulder to see if they were following and stopped dead, unable to believe my eyes. Monty, Jinks and Wellington were walking towards the gate right enough but they were walking *backwards*.

'Er, excuse me,' I called. 'Er, your ponies are walking backwards.' Hadn't they *noticed*? And where the hell was Jonathan with little Nancy?

61

I fished a piece of binder twine out of my pocket, tied Noah to the fence and hurried back up the yard. Tom, Tom and Sonia seemed to be performing a sort of quadrille in reverse and were making the oddest noises. I left them to it for the moment as I was puzzled about the disappearance of Nancy and Jonathan.

'Over here,' Nancy called, 'by the roses.' Jonathan had carted her into the front garden and was busily pruning a specimen camellia.

Stay calm, says the instructors' manual. So what if you've got three potty clients and three seemingly brain-damaged ponies. Not to mention a fearful scene when a certain someone finds the raped camellia. Stay Calm.

Motivated by the thought of £16, I stayed calm. There was no time to go indoors and consult my manual, and even if there was, what would I look up? Ponies stuck in reverse gear? I picked up Jonathan's reins and led him back to the yard. 'Sorry about that,' I said lightly. 'Jonathan's greed got the better of him. Shall we go?' I thought if I ignored the behaviour of Monty, Wellie and Jinks, they might come to their senses. No such luck.

'These ponies,' said Tom senior. 'Are they lame or something? They won't go forward.'

'Won't go forward?' I said in surprise. 'Whatever do you mean?'

'Stand back and I'll show you,' said Tom. He sat cowboy-style, with a loose rein, weight on the back of the saddle and legs braced forwards in the stirrups. Suddenly he said 'Ssss' and Monty, looking alarmed, began to back. Tom continued to say 'Ssss' and added a noise like 'Yuk yuk'. Monty went into a neat circle on the forehand.

'For Chrissakes stop him,' Tom laughed. I caught hold of Monty's bridle and held fast.

'Jinks and Wellington do that too,' said Sonia. 'They just won't go forward.'

'Have you ridden in England before?' I asked.

'No. We only got here last week. This is our first trip to Europe.' (Europe? I felt needled but kept calm.)

'Well, I think your American aids are confusing the ponies,' I said.

'You serious?' Tom drawled, and grinned at Sonia.

'Yes, of course I'm serious. Does "sss" mean "forward" where you come from?'

'Yeah. It means "get on fellah – let's go".'

'Ah, well, you see "sss" doesn't mean anything to an English pony. Nor does "yuk yuk". They probably think you're saying back back. Try sitting up straight so that your weight is in the middle of the saddle and say "walk on".'

To this day I don't know why they found the command 'walk on' so hysterically funny. They collapsed over their pommels every time they tried it. By now, of course, the ponies had got the upper hand and were pretending not to understand what 'wark arn' meant. They started to sidle back to their stables, at which point I lost confidence in the instructors' manual and produced three riding crops. 'Here,' I said handing them round. 'Hold the crop in your right hand and if any pony disobeys again, hit him firmly. Once should be enough.'

At last the ride was under way. Within a few minutes, both children had got the hang of maintaining contact through the reins and using their legs as well as their voices. Sonia took a little longer, but eventually convinced Jinks that Americans are not to be trifled with. ('We might not speak the same language, boy,' she told him, 'but *I'm* the one with the stick.') But poor Tom was not as adaptable as his wife and children. I have not made an international study of men's bottoms, but I think Americans must have bigger buttocks than Englishmen. Patently Tom's bum was in the wrong place, and it was my job to move it. Tricky.

'At least he's stopped going backwards,' Tom said. 'What the heck am I doing wrong?' He was such a nice man, probably an accomplished rider Western-style, but all at sea on a flat saddle.

'Try sitting about 6 inches further forward,' I said. 'At the moment all your weight is over Monty's kidneys and this inhibits a horse's impulsion.' I felt an absolute twit quoting from the book like that, and quite cross with the author for using flowery phrases. 'And sit up straight,' I added. That was plain enough. Tom squared his shoulders and pushed his hips forward sharply. A spasm of pain shot across his face and he clutched his groin. 'Ooh, heck,' he said (I think), followed by a few more oohs as Monty broke into a trot to catch up with the others. 'You OK, Tarm?' Sonia called back. 'Cute scenery huh?'

Tom looked far from well and spent most of the two-hour ride standing in his stirrups. Sonia and the children enjoyed themselves and wanted to book another session, but I felt sorry for Tom, and gave them the address of a Western riding school in North Devon.

For the first time in many moons the 'income' column in our Farmer and Stockbreeder Diary was putting up a brave fight against the 'outgoings' column. There was £12 from John for the Phyllishayes children's riding, £16 from the Americans, another £16 from individual rides and a nice, fat £30 from the sale of Richard piglet.

(Richard should really have earned us £50. He was the best boar we have ever bred; with his perfect conformation, eye-catching markings and friendly personality he would have made a good show pig, and we were intending to run him on for a few months in order to get a show-pig price for him. But when some ex-neighbours of my mother's – a young couple who taught rural studies in Hampshire – heard that we had a pedigree GOS boar, they wanted to buy him as a baby so that their pupils could watch him growing up. We jumped at the chance of such a good home for him, and off he went to Hampshire, where he became a much-loved pig and even had his picture in the local paper.)

But in the one week this year that there was more coming in than going out, Brian had to spoil it by paying a bill for straw and by putting a tenner's worth of diesel in the tractor. 'Why did you have to write it down?' I said crossly. 'You've ruined the look of it. Just this once we could have let income get to the bottom of the page first.'

Brian wasn't listening. He was making maternal noises over his trays of seed potatoes, which had been chitting in a spare bedroom and were now ready for action. 'Did you ever see so many shoots? And look at those Catriona – perfection. Will you and Anne give me a hand planting them?' I could see I wasn't going to be allowed to let my shoebox full of pound notes go to my head, so I closed the diary on that very satisfactory £74 entry and picked up a seed tray.

Brian had fenced the vegetable acre with pig netting stapled to 4 x 4-inch wooden posts. (The SHA owned and hired out a petrol-driven post-hole borer, which made a professional job of sinking shafts for the uprights.) It was the first time we had ever had a really stockproof fence; this one would have kept elephants out, but not, as we soon discovered, small dogs. Ella, Honey and Inky were too big to wriggle underneath, but Parsley and her year-old daughter, Melly, had no difficulty, and enthusiastically volunteered to plant potatoes too. Brian, who had spent weeks preparing seed beds, blew his top as both cavaliers raced round and round with potatoes in their mouths. 'I'll *kill* them,' he shouted. 'Why can't you two train the bloody things?'

'He's right, you know,' I said to Anne as we captured our endangered pets and tied them to a tree. 'They are terribly disobedient compared to the others. We ought to take them in hand.'

'It would take years to train Melly,' Anne said. 'She's rather dim.'

We carried on planting, row after row of Majestic, Catriona and Javelin, trowelling out a little hole for each potato and carefully lowering it in, sprouting side up. There were 28 lb of each variety, and we enjoyed the job, finding the smell of freshly turned earth a tonic after the long winter. The earth felt good too, nice and friable, full of goodness from the muck heap.

Anne went back to the house after a couple of hours, but instead of returning with a hoped-for cup of tea, she was carrying a roll of wire netting and a pair of pliers. 'Smaller mesh,' she explained, and proceeded to net the gap under the garden fence. Parsley and Melly were not too dim to realize that their gardening days were over, and when we untied them they went to sit with the others behind the netting, looking as sad as only spaniels can. Brian earthed up the last of the Majestics and started to collect the tools into an empty seed tray. 'These are my pliers, aren't they, Anne?'

'Yes. I found them on your kitchen table'.

'Did you shut the door?' Brian and I chorused. A silly question. Give Anne a door and she might sand it, paint it, or even rehang it, but never, never shut it. We hurried back to the house convinced that we should find at least one duck and probably six plopping all over our kitchen floor. The front garden gate was open, the front door and our kitchen door, but happily there was no evidence of ducks. Brian crossed the room to wash his hands at the sink, and I went to wash in the bathroom, which was a converted old dairy next to the kitchen. I pushed the door open about 6 inches and jumped with fright when a large, hairy face appeared in the crack.

'*Elizabeth*! Brian – Elizabeth's in the bathroom.' Brian towelled his face and swore he'd fix automatic closing devices on all the doors or take an axe to his mother-in-law. Neither of these alternatives was an answer to the immediate problem – how to make Elizabeth step backwards so that we could open the door wide enough to get her out.

The trouble was, she didn't want to come out. She had seen herself in the mirror and was quite happy to stay where she was, edged against the door, licking her reflection. Anne said wasn't it a pity she didn't have a friend, then she wouldn't have to look for one in the mirror. Luckily, cows are creatures of habit, and it wasn't long before her udder told her it was milking time. She lost interest in the mirror and let Brian persuade her to step back far enough to allow him to open the door. Fearing the worst, we peered in. But Elizabeth, like the perfect lady she was, had left no trace of her presence at all.

Chapter Seven

The SHA spring calendar was packed with meetings and courses. Those of us who had done the animal husbandry course in the autumn were now having the classroom lessons reinforced by practical work at Cannington College and at a nearby vet's surgery. We were also getting talks and demonstrations laid on by the SHA itself on a wide range of subjects – cheese-making, dog-handling, artificial insemination – you only had to name it and find a few other interested people and you had a course. Most were attended by ten or twelve people, sometimes as few as six if it was something like chain-sawing. We all found it was a myth that adults can't learn as quickly as children. Admittedly, we could have done with younger *bones*, but there was nothing wrong with our brains. Facts about parasitology, and The Law and the Landowner, were much easier to retain than the real mysteries of the universe, such as why the laundry basket is always full of unmatched socks.

One of the most interesting courses I went to was on lambing. A dozen or so of us spent a day practising being midwives to a 'phantom ewe', a metal and plastic contraption containing real lambs – dead ones provided by local farmers for students to learn on. The morning session started with the instructor placing a single lamb in the normal presentation position inside the ewe – the ewe's back lifted off to enable the instructor to keep her topped up with a succession of lambs – and we each in turn had to 'deliver' the lamb as quickly and carefully as we could. A ewe's pelvis is not very accommodating to the adult-sized hand, and the birth canal is quite a Beecher's Brook affair – up and over. If you kneel on the floor next to an ordinary kitchen chair – the sort with cross struts joining the legs – and try to ease a 10-lb weight over the strut using just two fingers, it will give some indication of the angle you have to adopt to

67

deliver lambs. It makes your knees and your back ache, and it's then that you wish you were a year or two younger.

After we had all delivered the 'normal' lamb to the instructor's satisfaction ('It's a good job this old girl's made of plastic,' he said, after one of us had caused her to give birth to her liver and kidneys as well), we had to do it again with a variety of malpresentations – breech, cord round neck and so on. At first it was hard to distinguish between a front hoof and a back hoof, but with practice we were able to work the tiny legs backwards and forwards to decide whether we were holding a knee or a hock.

A quick lunch in a nearby pub followed – *nobody* had roast lamb – then back to the ewe. Multiple births next. 'Twos, threes and fours,' said the instructor. Only he and the watchers knew how many he was posting in for each birth; the deliverer had to work it out by feel. 'Remember,' he said, 'however many you deliver, *always* go back in and look for another one. Even if she has six, look for seven.' The idea of looking for another one is misleading. You are feeling, with cramped fingers at the end of an aching arm inside what appears to be a rather knobbly football. Our language got a bit low as the afternoon wore on. 'I know you're in there, you buggers,' one of us shouted up into the ewe's vagina after several frustrating searches. 'Come out and be counted.'

When my first turn came I rolled up my sleeve and inserted my hand and arm up and over the now familiar pelvis. 'Eleven legs,' I said after a long exploratory session.

'Good,' said the instructor. 'And?'

'Two heads.' God, what sort of a monster was I going to deliver?

'Carry on,' said the instructor, 'you're a leg missing.'

'What about the third head?' someone asked.

'All in good time,' said the instructor patiently. I unravelled my triplets. Two of them were locked in such a close embrace that one lamb's head was sandwiched tightly between them, twisted back on its own shoulders. The twelfth leg put in an appearance too, much to my relief. Soon I had all three flopped out on the wet floor, pathetic little bodies which the instructor picked up by their back legs ready for another birth.

By the end of the day we were all quite good at extracting corpses from an unresisting mock-up mother. The test would come, our teacher said, when we tried to do it in pouring rain on an unco-operative live sheep.

Another enjoyable and instructive meeting was a one-day seminar on The Future of the Self-Sufficiency Movement, arranged by the SHA in conjunction with the Soil Association. Because it was thought that not many people would want to give up a warm spring day to come and listen to lectures, we booked only a small hall – Agriculture House, near Taunton – for the occasion. Brian and I were on the door selling tickets, and half an hour before the first talk was scheduled to begin, the hall was so packed that we had to send out for extra chairs.

The reason for the crowd was that we were lucky enough to have as guest of honour Major Sedley Sweeny, or God as someone called him. Sedley Sweeny was the acknowledged expert on small-acreage management. He had succeeded in doing what most of us were still dreaming about – making a living off a smallholding. In his case it was a very small holding of 10 acres that kept him and his wife in reasonable comfort. He had written many wise words about his experiences in running first the Tibetan Farm School in Wales, then his own project, and although most of us knew his current publication off by heart, we still wanted to see the great man in person.

He didn't fail us. He gave a long and interesting talk, starting with the whys of farming, and, having established a rapport with his audience, going on to describe his working year, month by month. He was a relaxed and witty speaker, and we lapped him up.

During the lunch break, while Sedley Sweeny and other guest speakers were being fed by some of our committee, the rest of us ate our sandwiches in the ornamental gardens of Agriculture House, and mingled with the Soil Association and members of the public. All the committee members were expected to circulate, mainly to drum up custom for the SHA and also to make new people feel welcome. Brian is very good at that sort of thing. He doesn't mind a quick encounter with a complete stranger; he's like a bee getting a bit of pollen out of each likely-looking flower. But as I am not good at it, I stayed with the familiar crowd and we mulled over the lecture. It had, we agreed, been both inspiring and daunting. 'He even does his own *welding*,' someone said enviously. (Sedley Sweeny had said any fool with land could feed his family; the clever thing was to learn to build and plumb, tile a roof, strip an engine...) 'He reminds me of an aunt of mine,' said another. 'During the war, when wool was rationed, she knitted herself a stair carpet out of old jumpers. He seems to be able to recycle anything too.'

The April sun had some real warmth in it and it was with some reluctance that we returned to the dim hall. Almost inevitably, the second speaker was a let-down. Although he had been briefed about the SHA and knew that we weren't absolute beginners, he addressed us as if we were turnip-tops. Our chairman for the day, a woman called Angela, was much kinder to him than he deserved. 'Why didn't she kick his teeth in for being so patronizing?' I hissed to Brian under cover of the small ripple of applause. 'She didn't need to. She's got a degree and he hasn't,' he whispered back. There was another brief lecture, then Sedley Sweeny returned to the platform for question time. We'd all have liked this to go on for ever, but Angela brought the meeting to an early end with the firmness of someone with animals waiting to be fed and milked. Quite funny considering how we had spent the day talking about the joys of being self-employed, free as air and so on.

Equipped now with the accumulated wisdom of highly qualified teachers, and with the confidence gained from practical experience, it should have been a piece of cake to go out and buy a pig or two. All you had to do was use four of your senses – look, feel, smell, listen – check its papers, if it had any, and you couldn't go wrong. However, it was only because the gods were on our side, for once, that our next purchase didn't go disastrously wrong.

I came indoors one day to find Brian saying 'Gloucester Old Spots' to someone on the phone. We had been promising ourselves more pigs for months now and I had almost given up, so this sounded promising.

'Sows, yes.' He screwed up his face to concentrate on what the other person was saying and jotted something down on a notepad. 'But, Mr Winter, whose sows are they? Not yours? Not hers? Sorry, I didn't quite catch...whose feet? Oh, your wife's feet. I'm so sorry. Look, this line's very bad. Can we come over and see you and discuss it? Yes, I've got a pencil – main road – Somerset – Minehead – fine. Straight away suit you? About an hour, then. Bye.' He put the phone down with a sigh of relief.

'Who was that?'

'I'm not sure. I couldn't understand half he was saying. It wasn't a bad line, but his accent was so Devonian, you know, all urghs and things, it sounded as though he had the phone in his pocket. His wife's feet aren't what they were, so he's cutting down on his pigs. At least I think that's what he said. But the pigs he's selling aren't actually his. Anyway, I said we'd go over and see him. It was Miss Kerr who gave him our number, so it should be OK.'

Miss Kerr was a remarkable, slightly eccentric old lady who had started us off on Gloucester Old Spots two years previously. Our Rose Hip, the mother of Briar and Bramble, had been bred by Miss Kerr, who still followed her progress closely. If Miss Kerr was recommending this other pig breeder, a Mr Winter, it probably meant he had good stock to sell.

Mr and Mrs Winter (he called her Mother and she called him Winter) welcomed us into their tiny cottage and sat us down tenderly, as if we had driven hundreds of miles to see them. Home-made cake awas pressed upon us and punishingly strong tea in half-pint enamel mugs. They were a lovely couple, fat and jolly, and with such broad accents that we found it quite hard to understand them. We did understand we were being grilled as to our suitability as potential pig-buyers, and very strange, too, it felt to be on the receiving end of this cross-questioning. How much land did we have, did we believe in infra-red lamps, did we believe in vets? (Vets baint be much good, they'm out to line their pockets.) In Mrs Winter I found a soulmate, a herbalist, no less, and an advocate of homeopathy. We chatted a while, then Mrs Winter started to clear the table. 'Winter'll show 'ee the pigs now. Dear souls,' she said. (The dear souls were the pigs, not us.) 'I'll stop in with my feet.' Her feet, which had given her good service for over eighty years, were beginning to wear out. The 'cropdisk' lady called once a fortnight and did whatever it is that cropdisk ladies do to aching feet, and she, Mrs Winter, musn't grumble.

Mr Winter led us outside and proudly introduced us to each of his eight pigs, housed in converted calf-pens with access to a small paddock beyond. A vet would have had a hard job to line his pocket here; the pigs were bursting with health and vitality. 'Which are the two you have for sale?' Brian asked.

'They'm not here. I told 'ee on the phone. Proper mimsy they are, poor mimsy wimsy dears. They'm in pig, mind, they've been indulledged.'

'In *Dulwich*?' I exclaimed. 'Oh, come off it, we're not going all the way to Dulwich to fetch a couple of pigs, surely…' I tailed off, silenced by a kick on the shin from Brian. 'Indulged,' he muttered under his breath, 'he means they've been indulged.' (Mr Winter was sparing my blushes by not saying 'mated'.)

'I slips 'un Wilfred for a couple o' days,' he went on. 'I'll show 'ee Wilfred; he'm a good begetter.'

I was so bowled over by Mr Winter's way with words that I quite lost the thread of his lengthy explanation about a brother-in-law and the whereabouts of our new pigs. I hoped Brian was paying attention so that he could tell me later. While they were talking, I scratched Wilfred, a friendly chap, and in good working order, too, judging by the dozens of little Wilfreds scurrying round our feet. Mr Winter sighed with pleasure at the sight of all his friends sunning themselves in the dusty yard and said it was better than teddies any road. I looked at Brian for a translation of 'teddies' and he mouthed 'potatoes', which left me none the wiser.

We went back to the house to say goodbye to Mrs Winter, then Mr Winter walked with us to the van. 'Remember,' he said, tapping the side of his nose, ''ee don't know nothing. *Nothing*. Nine o'clock Sat'day. Don't 'ee be late, mind.'

'Thanks, Mr Winter. Nine o'clock it is. Bye.' Brian slammed the door and we were off.

'Now,' I said. 'Are you going to wipe that silly grin off your face and let me in on the secret? Where are our pigs, why are they mimsy and wimsy and why all that cloak and dagger stuff about not knowing nothing?'

'We Devonians don't have any trouble understanding each other,' Brian began, He tapped the side of his nose. ''Ee don't know nothing, do 'ee?' I couldn't thump him because he was driving.

The story was quite straightforward once all the ers and uns and 'ees had been ironed out. Two months ago Mr Winter had sold two pigs for £50 each to his brother-in-law Herbert or 'Erb. (Small wonder I had lost the thread if there was an 'Erb in with all the other r sounds.) The pigs had been set to work ploughing up a piece of waste ground that 'Erb was renting from the council and on which he planned to grow a crop of potatoes. Too late, Mr Winter realized that 'Erb had no intention of keeping the pigs once the ground had been turned over, and was annoyed that someone, a relative at that, was using cheap pig labour instead of hiring a rotovator, so he offered to buy the pigs back. 'Erb wanted £50 each for them, but Mr Winter wasn't prepared to fork out £100 for what were now thin pigs (poor mimsy wimsy dears), especially as they were not pregnant. So he laid a plan.

For two consecutive days, under cover of darkness, he walked Wilfred, the friendly boar, along the road, across some railway lines and on to the piece of waste ground that the sows were ploughing. He waited while Wilfred 'indulledged' them, then walked him all the way home again. He then phoned Miss Kerr and asked her to find a good home for two pregnant pedigree GOS sows that would be going cheap. Meanwhile, he told 'Erb that although he didn't want pigs himself, he would be prepared to take them to Taunton market for 'Erb and get them auctioned for him. 'Erb, knowing that Mr Winter's reputation would enhance the price of any pig he put in, fell head first into the trap and agreed to let the pigs go to Taunton on Saturday morning.

'And that's where we come in,' Brian finished the tale. 'Nine o'clock sharp Saturday morning.'

'I still don't get it,' I said. 'How does Mr Winter know that we'll get them cheaply?'

'I haven't the faintest idea,' Brian admitted. 'He promised, that's all. We've got to pretend not to know him when we see him at the market.'

On Saturday morning we parked the van next to the pig-pens and strolled along the rows looking for two GOS sows in a single pen. There were Landrace, Welsh, Large White and even a couple of Tamworths, but no Spots.

'How disappointing,' I said, looking at my watch. 'His lorry must have broken down.'

'Mister.' A small boy tugged at Brian's sleeve. 'Mister, the man said look in number one.' And he melted back into the crowd. Evidently Mr Winter was watching us.

'Here's number one,' I said. 'Two Tamworths.' (Tamworths have apricot-coloured hair.) 'They're not, you know,' Brian said, leaning over the rail and rubbing one of the sleeping pigs. 'They've been painted.'

'Painted?' I lowered my voice, remembering our instructions – 'ee don't know nothing.

'Well, plastered then. He's plastered them with mud.'

'Good heavens! So he has.' I climbed into the pen to have a closer look, but before I had time to take in more than the fact that they were thin and dirty, the bell rang for the start of the sale. I hopped out quickly.

'Lot One, gentlemen,' said the auctioneer from his platform. 'Two plain sows.'

Plain sows? Whatever was Mr Winter playing at? (A 'plain' pig is one that is usually old, of no particular breed and definitely not pregnant.)

'What am I bid? Fifty someone? Forty? Start me at thirty-five, gentlemen.'

'Thirty,' said Brian casually. Nobody else even looked at the sleeping pigs (we found out later that Mr Winter had given them a huge breakfast to keep them lying down so that they looked smaller) and the hammer came down on Brian's opening bid. 'Both, sir? Thank you, sir,' said the auctioneer, and moved along the ledge to the next lot.

Brian and I looked at each other and burst out laughing. After all those hours spent taking notes on animal husbandry – the pig in sickness and in health – what *had* we done?

'I just hope there's nobody we know here,' Brian laughed. 'We'd never live it down. We haven't even seen them *awake* yet.' Mr Winter appeared and clapped Brian heartily on the back. 'We done it, my son, we done it,' he beamed. '£30! Hee, hee, hee – 'Erb won't have no more pigs in a 'urry, will un?' The last part of his revenge on poor old 'Erb had gone as planned. He had got to the market early and put them in pen number one, the only pen that was more or less guaranteed to attract no attention, as buyers liked to see what other people were going to do before they committed themselves. After a large feed, Mimsy and Wimsy (what else?) had buried themselves in the straw to sleep the morning away. Nobody looking at the two muddy yellow backs – the mud had come from 'Erb's own potato patch – would guess that they were looking at the pedigree daughters of a Ribbesford boar, one of the most sought-after studs in the country, or that they were in pig to the blue-blooded Wilfred.

'But "plain sows", Mr Winter?' I reminded him. 'Wasn't that going a bit too far? 'Erb must know they're pedigree pigs.'

''Erb never knowed about Wilfred,' said Mr Winter, avoiding the question with the skill of a politician, 'and it weren't my job to tell the auctioneer, were it? They'm not *my* sows.' He looked virtuously at the ceiling.

A few weeks later our 'cow wanted' advert in the SHA newsletter brought us Amelia, a two-year-old Jersey, due to calve in the autumn. This time we did everything right before buying her. We looked and listened, smelt her breath, felt her udder and checked her feet. Her registration papers showed that she was from an aristocratic line, her vet's certificate proved that she was pregnant, and her milking record was good. So we bought her, and very pretty she looked too, galloping round the fields with Elizabeth, who was delighted to have a new friend.

Milk records show how much milk a cow is giving. What they *don't* show is how willingly or otherwise the cow lets you have the milk, and Amelia made it plain from the start that unless she could dictate her own terms at milking time, we could whistle for it. She didn't like her south-facing stall and wouldn't eat from the stone manger. Most of all, she didn't like Radio 4. She didn't mind *Desert Island Discs*, but she really hated the shipping forcasts and the *Today* programme.

Brian let her have her own way for the first few days. He let stand back to front in her stall, fed her from a plastic bucket and turned the radio down low. Elizabeth had been dried off, so he had to humour Amelia or we wouldn't have had any milk. She was quite a madam, a real bossy boots. Her horns curved outwards like a Viking helmet and she was well aware of the extra authority this gave her. (Elizabeth had the opposite shaped horns, a gentle inward crescent shape, no threat to man or bucket.) Brian put up with her tantrums until she was giving a steady 3 gallons a day, then he took her in hand. We put pieces of hosepipe over the points of her horns, chained her up the right way round and put her nuts in the stone manger. Madam lashed out with her back leg in annoyance, so we tied her leg up, too. Reluctantly, she ate her food and let down a mere 1 gallon in revenge. (The act of eating triggers off a chemical reaction that makes a cow let down the milk.)

It took a week to get back to 3 gallons a day, and she always managed to have the last word, usually a jab in the back from her padded horns. She wasn't a bad character out of the milking parlour, but she liked having her own way. If we could have persuaded the BBC to broadcast *Desert Island Discs* twice a day, seven days a week, Amelia would probably have doubled her milk yield. As it was, Brian looked forward to June, when Elizabeth and he could resume their companiable milking times, listen to the six o'clock news together and discuss current affairs like civilized men and cows.

Chapter Eight

'Saw W coming back ag'. This was the note by the telephone in Anne's small, neat writing. It could have been in Chinese for all the sense it made. We had just come in for morning coffee, and Anne had gone out for a walk with the dogs. 'Who's W?' I said.

'Search me. Who's ag come to that?'

'AG could be her initials. Anne Gordon.'

'Don't be ridiculous,' said Brian testily. 'Why would your mother sign her name on a phone message? We know who she is.'

'I've got it,' I said triumphantly. 'Look, the pencil's broken. She was writing ag when the lead snapped. I bet it means "W is coming back again."'

'How can anybody come back again unless they've already been?' Brian argued.

'Perhaps it's the man to read the meter, or swallows.'

'Swallows?'

'Mm. That W looks like a flying bird. I think she's seen the swallows coming back to the barn. She wouldn't want us to miss that. Anyway, I must fly too. I've got that ghastly Mrs Prentice and Lalage at twelve o'clock. See you at lunchtime. Bye.'

Mrs Prentice was persevering with Lalage's riding lessons, even if Lalage was not. I had to admire the old battleaxe's staying power. Lalage had made no progress at all, but Mrs P was convinced that there was an improvement because Lalage had not yet fallen off. I made jolly sure she didn't fall off by always putting her on the reliable Wellington. We would plod round bridle paths for an hour, which was just long enough to put some colour into Lalage's cheeks. Mrs Prentice seemed to think she was getting her £2 worth if Lalage returned slightly breathless, so we would ride the last few minutes at a trot, with me willing Lalage to stay in the saddle. I didn't feel too bad about her lack of progress because she simply wasn't interested in riding, and nobody can force a child to learn something that doesn't interest them. I shouldn't be sorry, though, when Mrs Prentice found something else for Lalage to try.

She was waiting for us as usual when we got back. I called out hello and wondered what theme she would choose for today's sermon. (Five minutes' mild bullying time was a pretty fair exchange for £2 in view of the fact that I wasn't really giving Lalage value for money.

'Laburnums,' she barked, as if reading my mind. 'Don't you know laburnum trees are deadly poisonous?' I helped Lalage to dismount and led Noah and Wellie into their stables. Mrs P followed.

'You'll have to chop it down,' she continued, blocking the light by standing in the doorway.

'Chop what down, Mrs Prentice?'

'That laburnum tree in your front garden. It'll have to go.'

'I didn't know we had a laburnum tree. We moved here during the winter.' I handed Lalage the two bridles to take to the tack-room, and slung the two saddles over my arm. 'But thanks for telling me. I'll make a note of it.' I wouldn't, of course, but it was often much simpler to let her run out of steam, and with luck she might have Lalage into scuba-diving by the time the laburnum blossomed.

Mrs Prentice changed the subject abruptly. 'One of your labourers was rather insolent to me this morning.'

'Oh, I'm sorry to hear that.' (I'll *kill* Brian if he's been pulling the leg of a Regular Client.)

'You must speak to him. It doesn't do to let these types answer back. They get ideas. Well?'

'Er, well what?'

'Don't you want to know what he *said*? How can you tick him off if you don't know what he said?'

'I'll find a way,' I promised sincerely.

'I said to him – grubby beast…two years' conscription would

do these people the world of good – I said, "Have you been beating that dog?" and he had the cheek –'

'Which dog?' I interrupted.

'Your dear little whippet, the elderly one.' Mrs Prentice surprisingly had a genuine love of all animals and birds. 'She was crawling along on her belly, positively cringing. She'd obviously been beaten.'

'Oh, that's just her act. Honey always cringes. She's been like that from a small puppy and she's never been beaten.'

'I tell you she *has*. She...'

'Excuse me.' Brian loomed in the doorway, no grubbier or beastlier than usual.

'This is my husband, Brian,' I said. 'I believe you've, er, already met?'

'No,' said Mrs Prentice. 'How do you do?'

'How do you do? Enjoy your ride, Lalage? Sorry to interrupt, but we've got surprise visitors for lunch.'

'Visitors?' I said. This must be Anne's mysterious W.

'Lalage and I will be off, then,' said Mrs Prentice. 'Don't forget to have a word with your man.'

'No, I won't.' I closed the tack-room door and hurried towards the house. 'Who is it, Brian? Who *is* W?'

'It as an M. It's Marcus.'

'*Marcus*? Oh, how lovely.'

'And Andy. They're on a flying visit.'

Marcus and Andy, who had known each other from primary school days, were spending the weekend moving Andy into a rented cottage in Bristol, where he was on a university sandwich course. Over a strictly non-meat lunch – Marcus was a vegetarian and Andy was thinking of going over – we heard all their news. Marcus, who had taken a temporary job at children's holiday camp in Wales the previous year, had liked it so much that he had joined the permanent staff. The accommodation at the camp was a bit cramped for all his books and noise-making equipment, so he had joined forces with Andy and another lad called Vernon to rent a cottage in Bristol as a base for the three of them.

'We finished unloading Andy's stuff quite early,' Marcus

said, 'and as we've got the loan of a car for the whole weekend, we thought we'd surprise you. Then, on the way here, we got a slow puncture, so we bombed in, left a message with Anne that we'd come back after twelve, then took the car to a garage. No spare tyre, you see.'

The boys finished their soup and made triple-decker cheese and peanut butter sandwiches, which Marcus said were Andy's speciality as he was on a sandwich course.

'You don't improve, do you?' I said. 'And that reminds me, which of you has been offending my customers this morning?'

'He has.' They pointed at each other and laughed. 'Was that Amazon a friend of yours, then?'

'No, of course not. Her daughter comes to ride. She said one of you was insolent – 'a grubby beast' was the actual description, and that could be either of you.'

'She'd be grubby if she'd been pumping up a car tyre every half-hour,' said Marcus indignantly.

'She wouldn't have to use a pump, she could blow it up by mouth.' Andy choked on his triple-decker at the thought. Brian thumped him on the back and said it served him right.

'She said you answered back,' I persisted.

'Well, of course we answered back,' Marcus giggled. 'If someone asks you a question, you answer, don't you? She said, "Have you been beating that dog?" so naturally I said, "Yes, I have, but she wasn't really trying." Good one, eh?'

'Oh, Marcus,' said Brian disapprovingly, 'that joke was ancient when I was a boy. We'll have to get you kitted out with some fresh material.'

After lunch, Anne took the boys off to look round, while Brian helped me with some leading-rein toddlers who needed a reassuring arm around them for their first rides. When we got back, Marcus and Andy had decided to stretch their flying visit into an overnight stay. Anne had told them all about her parachute-jumping project, and they were thrilled to bits at the idea of an SAS-type granny; so marvellous, they thought, not to let age get in the way of achievement. They rigged up a practice platform for her in an apple tree with straw underneath to make a soft landing, and spent an hour or so testing it out themselves.

At bedtime, Anne and I made up two beds for them in a spare room that up till now had not been used, except for chitting potatoes. We all said goodnight and went off to bed. In the morning, when I went to wake the boys with a cup of tea, I found the beds had not been slept in and were minus their blankets and pillows. How odd, I thought, and retraced my steps.

I discovered them in another bedroom, curled up on mattresses on the floor wrapped up in the missing blankets. 'Morning,' I said, poking at the nearest body with my foot. They were indistinguishable in the half-light, their shoulder-length air cascading off the pillows. 'What are you doing in here?'

One of them sat up and groped for his face through the jungle creeper. It was Andy. 'Ghost,' he said. 'What's the time?'

'Half past seven. What do you mean, ghost?'

'*Half past seven?*' he said in disbelief. 'In the *morning?*' Quite extraordinary really to think of the years you spend trying to get kids to stay *in* bed, then the same number of years trying to get them out again.

Marcus surfaced. 'Tea?' he said. If he had to confront such a hideous notion as 7.30 a.m., he needed his shot first. I put the mugs down between the mattresses. 'What's all this about a ghost?'

It seemed the bedroom where they had started the night was already occupied by a man (they were both sure it was a man) who was shut in a cupboard. 'He kept knocking on the door,' Marcus said. 'We couldn't get to sleep.'

'We opened the cupboard door,' Andy added, 'and he knocked on it where it wasn't, if you see what I mean. So we moved our things in here.' As they had had nothing stronger than cocoa the night before, I told them they were both daft and it was about time they grew up.

Later in the day, when they had more of their wits about them, we all went to investigate the knocking cupboard. It was a perfectly ordinary-looking cupboard, empty, thick with dust and cobwebs, with a wooden door and a metal catch. The only thing that was different about that particular room was that it had a small spiral staircase leading down to a sitting-room on the ground floor. It might have been a priest's hole. The deeds of the house went back to the sixteenth century, but we couldn't understand the early ones as they were written in medieval Latin.

Marcus and Andy went back to Bristol and we resumed our normal gardening/riding/parachute-practising day. That night I asked Brian if he would sleep in the ghost's room with me. I wasn't afraid of the ghost because I didn't then believe he was there, but I was afraid of the spiders that I knew were there. Brian, as conservative as Amelia, refused to leave the comfort of his own bed to spend the night in a bleak room full of spare furniture. Anne wouldn't either because there was nowhere to plug in a bedside lamp.

Armed with two hot-water bottles, a book and a Flit gun, I decided to go it alone. Settling down in one of the beds, I read for a while, then got out of bed, switched off the light and got back in again. I must have been asleep only a few minutes when the knocking started: rat tat tat...ratty tat...knock knock knock. Strangely enough it was not in the least bit scary, just annoying. I got out of bed and put the light on. The knocking stopped. Aha, I thought, an electrical fault. Ghost indeed. But soon the knocking started again, with the light on now. 'Shut up,' I yelled. There were a few more raps, then silence.

I stayed in the room about an hour. Sleep was out of the question. The knocking wasn't regular, just a flurry every twenty minutes or so. Even with the cupboard door open, it was just as Andy had said; the noise seemed to come from the space where the door would have been when shut. So I gave up and went back to my own bed. Brian's language, when my freezing feet touched him, cheered me up no end. There wasn't a trace of medieval Latin about it, just plain Anglo-Saxon.

The mystery of the ghost had to remain unsolved. We had enough to think about without becoming agony aunts to some sixteenth-century misfit who'd got himself lost in time and space, so beyond sending the deeds to a brainy friend in London for translation, we did nothing.

The grass was growing ahead of the stock, which is to say there was too much for the number of animals eating it. All the ponies had to be grass-rationed, coming into their stables by day and being allowed to graze only during the night. Gorging on early summer grass can cause laminitis, a disease of the hoof, which is as painful to ponies as having a large splinter under a fingernail would be to a human. Elizabeth and Amelia, and the three orphan lambs, Johnny, Cleo and Ramrod, were literally in clover, fetlock deep in 12 acres of permanent pasture. All the pigs and piglets were folded in the apple orchard, which was a nice arrangement as the trees gave them shade while they kept the grass down.

We shut up about 6 acres for hay and decided to buy sheep to follow the grazing rotation of the cows and ponies. Sheep are nature's hoovers; they eat up all the rubbishy bits that the other animals leave, including parasite larvae, with no ill-effects to themselves. In a moment of insanity, we bought six Jacob ewes with ten lambs between them. Jacobs' wool is much sought after by spinners and weavers, of which there were many in the SHA, and it was partly the thought of having plenty of outlets for the wool and partly because they were on the Rare Breeds list that we chose them. We had had them only ten minutes when it became apparent *why* they were on the Rare Breeds list.

Tony was shoeing some of the ponies when Brian drove into the yard with the sheep in the back of the Transit.

'Jacobs?' he said incredulously. 'You don't mean you've gone and bought *Jacobs*?'

'We needed a few sheep to keep the grass down,' I said. 'They'll eat the long stuff that the ponies and cows leave.'

Tony snorted. 'They won't, you know. Damn things never stay still long enough to eat anything. Why didn't you buy Suffolks or Southdowns? Those maniacs taste like shoelaces.'

'We shan't be breeding for meat. Obviously, the ram lambs will go for meat, but all we want them for is the wool.'

Brian got out of the van looking dazed and smelling strongly of lanolin. 'Enjoy your drive, Brian?' Tony said casually.

'No,' said Brian. 'It was like hell in there. I had to keep all the windows shut to stop them jumping out. They're on the frisky side.'

'Tony says they're maniacs and they taste like shoelaces.'

'Always were a ray of sunshine, weren't you, Tony? If I back the van up to the stable door, can you two get them into the stable? We'll check them over, then turn them out in a field.'

Tony collected up his shoeing tools and stowed them neatly in the back of his van, while Brian backed the Transit a few yards. I thought we were going to carry the lambs out with their anxious mothers following at our heels, but evidently the Jacob ewes had not read the same textbooks as I had.

As soon as the back doors were opened, all six of them catapulted out into the stable and started leaping around like March hares. Tony shut the lower half of the stable door, then, before we knew what was happening, two of the ewes hurtled through the air over the top of the door and shot off towards Taunton. 'Top door – quick,' said Tony urgently, but I was too late. A third ewe flew over our heads and was gone, leaving Brian, who had tried a flying tackle, sprawled on the ground. Tony buried his face in his handkerchief, his shoulders shaking.

'Haven't you got anybody else's horses to shoe today?' asked Brian pointedly. Tony said he didn't mind hanging on a bit to give us a hand. Then Anne came out of the house with three mugs of tea and five dogs.

'I heard bleating,' she said, peeping through the mesh of the top stable door. 'Aah, aren't they *sweet*? What pretty coats – all different colours. Why have you shut them in?'

'They're going to count them,' Tony said, straightfaced. 'Some of them seem to have gone missing.'

'Three ewes escaped,' I explained. We drank our tea and wondered what would be the best way to catch them. Tony said they would probably come back if they heard their own lambs calling, but Anne thought it would be quicker to let Ella round them up and drive them. 'After all she is a collie,' she said, 'and she's used to the orphan lambs.'

'She doesn't know she's a collie, though,' I objected.

'Then this is a good time for her to learn,' Anne said.

'Come on, Ella, come and be a sheepdog.' All four of us, plus the five dogs and a lamb I fished out of the stable, marched down the road to look for the migrating ewes.

Chapter Nine

The odds against the lamb I was carrying being the offspring of one of the three ewes were very long indeed. We found the sheep cropping the grass verge about 100 yards down the road and I put the lamb down near them, having first made him a collar and lead out of binder twine. He bleated and struggled like a fish on a line. Ella trotted over to comfort him. All three ewes raised their heads, stamped their forefeet and charged at Ella angrily. Ella took one look at them and dashed any hopes we might have had of seeing her on *One Man and His Dog*. She fled.

'Nice-*looking* dog,' said Tony kindly. I picked up the lamb and walked backwards, hoping that at least one of the ewes would follow, but they went on grazing. Brian, Anne and Tony circled behind them and inched them on to the road and in this fashion we reached the yard and shut the gate.

Getting them into the stable without letting the others out was impossible, so we drove them into the open-fronted hay-barn and tied a tubular metal gate across to block the exit. Again, we witnessed the astonishing sight of fully grown sheep leaping through the air like kangaroos: they cleared the gate effortlessly, then orbited round the stable-yard in a frenzy. Just as Ella didn't know she was a collie, they didn't know they were sheep. Tony and Brian fetched a couple of walking sticks and hooked two sheep round the necks. I grabbed one by the horns and, to my surprise, one of the horns came away in my hand. Anne picked it up, examined it and said she would try later to stick it back on with Araldite.

Tony, who seemed to be starting a cold, helped to pen the sheep in another stable with a top door, before driving away to his next shoeing appointment. Anne coaxed Ella out of the house and took her to look for the other dogs who had slipped off on a rabbiting spree when we weren't looking.

'A breather next, I think,' said Brian. We sank down on the wooden seat in the front garden and were immediately joined by the three orphan lambs, who had evidently been keeping out of the way of the commotion in the yard. They were supposed to live in the paddock next to the house, but spent most of their time by the garden gate, counting the minutes until bottle-time came round. They were growing quite fast, as well they might on undiluted Jersey milk, and were much too heavy to sit on our laps. 'You're going to be part of a flock now,' I told them. 'You must teach those Jacobs how to behave.' Ramrod sucked at Brian's frayed shirt collar and fell asleep with it in his mouth, so I crept indoors for the camera.

Three-quarters of our large collection of photographs are of animals *not* doing cute things. By the time you've found the camera and set the light meter, your subject has stopped standing on its head or whatever, and is just being a puppy or a duck or a lamb. I therefore took a picture of Ramrod *not* sucking the shirt collar, then it was time to get to grips with the Jacobs again.

All we had to do to them at this time of the year was trim their hooves and cut away the thick wool under their tails. Dipping, shearing and worming would come later, July maybe, even August, depending on the weather. Brian caught them one at a time and held them in a vice-like grip between his knees while I cut the mucky wool away with scissors. (If you don't keep them clean around the rear, flies lay eggs in the dirty fleece and the sheep becomes a walking maggot factory.) Then we up-ended them and gave each hoof a pedicure with a sharp penknife, scraping out the dirt in the cleft of the foot, cutting back overgrown horn tissue and finishing off with an antiseptic foot spray. As we released each sheep, it went crazy, invigorated by the feel of nice, clean feet. Round and round the stable they bounded, crashing into walls and us and losing a few more pieces of their horns in the process.

'We should have set their blasted feet in concrete, not freshened them up,' said Brian, wincing as someone's head connected with his shins. To get them out of the stables and into the field, we decided to take each one separately on a dog's collar and lead. It must have looked daft, but anything was better than risking them whizzing round our heads again.

First we carried all ten lambs out to the furthest end of the furthest field, then we hauled the first protesting ewe out of the stable. She was surprisingly strong and pulled me over. 'Hang on to her,' Brian yelled. He shut the stable door, took the lead from me and sat on her head. That kept her still long enough for me to fetch a rope, which we tied round her neck so that now we had her doubly secured. She glared at us but realized she was well and truly captive and might as well give in.

It was hardly any trouble to frogmarch her to the group of lambs, although by the time we had done the journey six times, we were sorry we had put them so far away. At last, peace descended. All the ewes found their lambs and settled down to graze, building up their strength for the next round against the nasty humans. We tried to introduce Johnny, Cleo and Ramrod into the flock, but they didn't like the Jacobs any more than we did, and followed us all the way home again.

We now had a situation that Konrad Lorenz might have found useful for a thesis to the Royal Society (Identity Confusion in Farm Animals), but that was not what we had planned. There were sixteen sheep who thought they were yoyos, a collie who ran away from sheep, three lambs who thought they were humans, and, for good measure, a cat who thought she was a dog. There was nothing we could do about Small's problem, which, in any case, was quite harmless, but *surely* we should be able to train Ella to behave true to type? We looked through the local paper and found that there were dog-training classes held weekly in a village hall some 6 miles away. Ella, it was decided, should go to school.

For the first lesson I thought I had better take Parsley too, just to give Ella some moral support. Ella was only a year old and had led a sheltered life. She liked to play with visitors' dogs, but I didn't know how she might react to a village hall full of barking strangers. We arrived at 7.30 p.m., which was the time given in the advertisement, and found a stream of people and dogs leaving the hall.

'Excuse me,' I said to the man on the door. 'Have I come at the wrong time? It said seven-thirty in the paper. I want to start obedience classes.'

'Seven-thirty is for show training,' said the man, 'the obedience training is six-thirty to seven-thirty, then the show class starts. My word, what beautiful dogs. You'll be wanting to show them, surely?'

'I did intend to show them when we bought them,' I admitted, 'but there never seems to be enough time to go to shows.'

'Well, now that you're here why not try a show class? It's great fun and no training is wasted, is it?'

'Yes, I think I will,' I said. 'How much is it?'

'Ten pence for you and five pence each for the dogs. You can get coffee later and there's a raffle at the end.'

I paid up with a flourish. it seemed very reasonable for private education. Ella whined and hung back but Parsley was eager to see what all the racket was and tugged at her lead impatiently. In side was an atmosphere of controlled chaos with dogs barking and owners rearranging the chairs to form a huge circle. Everybody was welcoming to me and a few other first timers. 'Tie your spare dogs to the radiators,' one of the organisers called, and then when he saw the size of some of the dogs, amended it to 'Tie your *small* dogs to the radiators, please.'

Ella and Parsley were in different classes but the routine was more or less the same. Everybody had to parade their dog in a large circle then make it stand still while the judge looked at each one separately. The bigger dogs stayed on the floor and the small ones were examined on a table. Parsley positively enjoyed all the attention and Ella, once ahe realised nobody was going to bite her, stopped pretending to be a floorboard. It was quite good fun; the other people were very friendly and all the dogs seemed to like being part of a pack.

A woman with a cavalier puppy came up to me during the coffee break and gazed at Parsley intently. 'That's *got* to be Larry's daughter,' she said. 'I can see Richard in the eyes, but I'd know Larry's head anywhere.'

'Oh, I don't think she could be related to yours,' I said. I don't come from Devon. I bought Parsley from a breeder near London three years ago.'

'What's her pedigree?'

I rattled off the names of Parsley's sire line back four generations. I have an elephant's memory for useless information, but so seldom meet anybody to impress with this minor accomplishment that I wasn't going to waste this opportunity. I could also have told her how many earthworms there were to a square acre of Wiltshire chalkland, but she didn't ask.

'I knew it,' she said, before I could start on the maternal ancestry. 'I bred Richard and Larry – her grandfather and father. Richard was one of my best dogs. I've got just the stud for you.' I warm instantly to people who make me offers like that. We took our coffee to a quietish part of the hall and introduced ourselves.

My new friend's name was Leoni. She was a judge of spaniels and a breeder of cavaliers. One of her dogs, Larry, had been sent to stud at the breeder's where I had bought Parsley. The chances of meeting Parsley's co-breeder in a small village hall in Devon must have been astronomically remote. But the coincidences didn't stop there; they never do. Leoni also had a daughter called Sarah (with an h and married) and, oddest of all, lived not a mile from Taunton.

'We live about 6 miles out. I suppose you're an expert in commercial horticulture, too?' I said jokingly.

'Not an expert,' said Leoni, 'but I did have a tomato and lettuce nursery in Essex before I moved to Devon.' She said she brought her young, inexperienced dogs to the village classes to accustom them to show procedure. 'Is that why you're here?' she asked. 'To start Ella and Parsley off?'

I explained how I had got the times wrong but would probably come to this class again. It was nice meeting doggy people who went to shows for fun rather than cups, and Ella's shepherding lessons could probably be done at home from a book. Leoni thought I should enter Parsley for a forthcoming show that was being held about 20 miles away.

'Oh, I don't know,' I said, suddenly getting cold feet. 'It's one thing larking about in a village hall, but a big show? I'm bound to trip over the lead.'

'Don't be daft. Parsley's a super little dog and you know it. She's got every chance of being in the first three, and it will be interesting for you to see how the professionals, um, how *professional* some people can be.' We exchanged phone numbers, then Leoni took her young dog home before the second session as she didn't want to overtax it on a first outing.

It was funny to see how Ella reacted to the first session at school. When we got home, she did what many children do: she refused her dinner, climbed into bed and crashed out until morning. An hour spent in concentrated brainwork, plus the excitement of being with other dogs, had exhausted her. Parsley, a tougher personality altogether, ate both dinners, then showed off to Brian and Anne, leaping on and off the furniture for the rest of the evening. 'I think she's telling us something,' Anne laughed.

'She is too. OK, Parsley, I'll take you to the show.'

On the morning of the show I bathed Parsley and she added her own dab of Dior by rolling in cow muck just before we left. There wasn't time to bath her again so I put a wet sponge and a towel in the car. She was only entered in a novice class, after all, and the judge would probably be used to farmyard cologne.

When we arrived at the show, I saw to my astonishment that Parsley was the only cavalier who walked in on her own paws. All the others were being carried in wire-mesh cages. The owners, mainly women, greeted each other with pseudo heartiness, but nobody said hello to me or what a nice dog or anything. Parsley and I found a seat and shared a few choc drops to give us Dutch courage.

The first class to be judged was the puppies, and while this was in progress, the 'novice' owners (our class) began to get their dogs ready. My eyes nearly fell out when I saw the paraphernalia they had brought with them: vanity cases full of brushes, combs, eye-drops, *nail varnish*, oils and chamois leathers. It made my wet sponge look a bit feeble, and I wished we hadn't come. After half an hour, the puppies left the ring and the steward called the novices in. 'Come on, Parsnips,' I said. 'Show the flag. We'll have the rest of the choc drops afterwards.'

The class was huge, twenty-five altogether, mainly Blenheims, with eight tricolour and one ruby. My spirits rose when I saw the opposition. I hadn't had a chance to look at them properly when they were being tarted up. Parsley was clearly the second best dog in the ring; the best was a ruby-coloured one with a lovely, compact body, straight movements and a beautiful silky ruff. It was a male, which can be a slight advantage in a mixed class, as they tend to have thicker coats. We all paraded our dogs for a while, then lined up while the judge examined each dog on the table.

At the village-hall training class this waiting time was the chance for a natter with one's neighbours, so I assumed this would be the same at a real show. Turning to the woman next to me, who, in my opinion, had the third best dog, I said, 'Crummy lot, aren't they?'

'I beg your pardon? she said stiffly, and gathered her dog nearer to her feet.

'I said crummy lot. Apart from yours, mine and the ruby, there's not one here that you could call a show standard cavalier.'

'A judge, are you?' she sneered. 'An expert?' She looked at Parsley's fur: 'Your dog's got an infection.'

'Cow muck actually. She rolled in it just before we left home.'

We waited in an uncomfortable silence while the table judging went on. Leoni had told me how the breed standard had deteriorated in recent years (it often does when a breed becomes popular), and I could see exactly what she meant. The main fault with nearly all the dogs was that they were too big. Kennel Club standard weights for cavaliers is 15 lb for a bitch and 18 lb for a dog, but some of these were nearer 25 lb. Even the smaller ones were poor specimens, the result of unselective breeding by the get-rich-quick brigade.

Parsley went on the table and greeted the judge like a long lost friend. This I knew would lose her some marks. 'Sorry,' I said. The judge, a friendly woman who looked a bit like a spaniel herself, said not to worry, but *what* was that green on Parsley's fur? Oh, cripes, I thought, that's some more marks gone. Then I had to trot her up and down before taking my place at the end of the queue.

After all the dogs had been seen, we had to run them round more while the judge stood in the middle. She called in the ruby first, then Parsley, then my toffee-nosed neighbour, then a little tricolour that was the least bad of a runty-looking bunch. She handed the red rosette to the ruby's owner, then went into a huddle with her steward to decide whether Parsley or Toffee-Nose should be second.

'Will you trot them again, please? Side by side this time,' she said. The two dogs started down the strip of matting in the ring but by the time we reached the turn the other woman had managed imperceptibly to inch Parsley right off the mat and on to the bare floor. It was rather cleverly done and as we ran back (with Parsley still off the mat) I said to her: 'I see you've studied Stephen Potter,' but she just looked ahead and didn't answer.

The judge handed her the second prize and me the third. 'She's a grand dog,' she said, 'but her ringcraft is rather poor.'

'Yes, it is,' I agreed, 'and mine's not up to much, is it?'

The judge smiled. 'You'll learn,' she said. 'You'll learn.'

But I came to the conclusion as I watched the rest of the show that dog-showing was a hobby that could wait until I was old and rich. It is very time-consuming – exhibitors are not allowed to leave the premises until after the show – and no fun unless there is keen competition. I wouldn't have had the judge's job for anything. Leoni told me later that a judge is allowed to withhold the top prizes if the standard is too low to merit an award, but, of course, if they do do this, they have to be pretty thick-skinned to withstand the stream of abuse from disgruntled losers.

'It was interesting,' I told Brian and Anne over dinner the same evening, 'but not a lot of fun. I'd give it three out of ten.' We have a scale of values for leisure activities: they have to be either stimulating, instructive, amusing or lucrative, and a score under five means we might dabble with it again one day, but probably not.

Ella, who was the cause of all this doggy interest, continued to play happily with Ramrod, Cleo and Johnny, and to flee from the horned Jacob mothers. In time Cleo and Johnny joined the Jacobs and became proper sheep, but Ramrod refused to be weaned from his beloved bottle and hung around the house for another full year. We used to tie him on a running link to the clothes-line whenever we went out or he would run after the car, bleating pathetically at being left behind. He was a real pest, but he was also growing into such a good-looking ram (he was a Dorset Horn) that we decided to keep him for breeding instead of eating him. The fact that we were fond of him might have had something to do with the decision.

Chapter Ten

At the beginning of June, during a spell of hot weather, Brian's rooted chrysanthemum cuttings arrived. (In a Securicor van of all things; apparently it's cheaper than the post.) He had prepared a site for them, so as soon as we had given them a long drink after their journey, we started planting. On the first day we planted 625. Never has a day seemed so long. Each plant had to be eased out of its polythene envelope, lowered carefully into a dibbed-out hole, firmed in with two thumbs and finally watered by hand. If there had been a piped water supply to the field, it would have saved quite a lot of time, but there was only a natural stream running alongside a hedge. Every ten plants or so, we took the watering cans to the stream, filled them from a jug and carted them back to the plants. We felt like gibbons by the end of the day with all that squatting and water carrying, and even hot baths didn't unkink our spines.

On the morning of the second day Brian informed us cheerfully that professional nurserymen planted by the thousand per head per day. I managed to get a few minutes' non-planting time by challenging this absurd claim and starting an argument. Brian produced his book of words. The unspeakable nurserymen did indeed plant by the thousand. They had automatic irrigation systems too. Anne and I hoped they would all die slow lingering deaths, preferably by trowel or dibber. By 10 a.m. we were at it again, planting and watering, hour after back-breaking hour.

'Thirteen hundred and seventy five,' Brian announced at 6.30 p.m. 'They seem to have sent us 10 per cent extra with each packet, I ordered 1250. Don't the rows look neat?'

'Lovely,' I lied. Each row was 50 yards long, but as I was now bent double, with no immediate hope of straightening up, I couldn't actually see much beyond my own feet. 'If that's the lot, Brian, I vote we get a Chinese take-away to celebrate. I don't think I could reach the stove this evening.' Brian said he didn't think *planting* was an occasion for celebration, but agreed that a Chinese take-away was a good idea. He offered to do all the feeds as well as the milking if I would go and buy it.

When I got to town, I was surprised to see quite a few tractors parked in the High Street outside the fish and chip shop and the Chinese restaurant. Farm labourers, who had now started to get an early cut of hay while the weather was good, were buying take-away meals to eat in the fields before resuming an evening stint of haymaking. There was a wonderfully friendly feeling in the queue as sweat-streaked men called to each other. "Ow's it going then, Willum?' 'Got nigh on 10 ton off me 6-acre.' '£11 for a linkage pin! I sez, look, mister, I don't want ter buy a whole bloody tractor, I sez, just a linkage pin.'

The men bought chips to go with sweet and sour pork, pancake rolls, chow mein and prawn curries. Some had brought their sheepdogs for a meal, too, and asked the assistant for spare ribs without the sauce and some chips, 'not too hot, please, hot chips makes 'un sneeze'. The smell in the shop was intoxicating – a lovely mixture of cut grass, men's sweat and fried batter, three of my favourite things. I shouldn't have been at all surprised if the men had started a rousing chorus of 'To Be a Farmer's Boy' – it was that sort of gathering.

While we were eating our Chinese meal, Brian dropped a casual hint that there might be a bit more planting tomorrow.

'Bit?' Anne and I sat up as straight as our sciatic nerves allowed and looked at him accusingly. 'Not *more* chrysanths, Brian, you said that was the lot.'

'Cabbage plants, actually,' Brian said. 'Only 500.'

Anne, choking on a prawn cracker, said: 'Five hundred cabbages? For *three* people?'

'For the cows' winter feed,' explained Brian. 'They're cheap at the moment – only 2 pence each – and I want to get them in before we start haymaking. We don't have to plant them as carefully as the chrysanths, you know. They can be laid in the trench and earthed in with the back of a rake. Hardly any bending.'

'You make it sound like a rest cure,' I said, 'but what about watering?'

'I'll do all the watering,' he promised. 'We should be able to do it in half a day.' It would be his birthday tomorrow, and if he wanted to spend it toiling in the blistering sun, we could hardly refuse to help.

When, last thing at night, we went out to shut the chickens up and check that everything was in its rightful paddock or stable, we found Elizabeth was dripping with milk. Her calf was not due for another week, but we decided not to take any chances (she had lost her previous calf due to our ignorance and stupidity) and fetched a torch to examine her thoroughly. Her pin-bones had dropped and she was restless. That could mean the calf was on its way, but her vulva was tight and firm, which indicated nothing was likely to happen for a few hours yet. Amelia's behaviour was very odd. She kept licking Elizabeth's back, rasping her long tongue along the spine, always towards the tail – a kind of bovine version of the massage husbands are encouraged to give their wives.

'Let's get to bed for a couple of hours,' Brian said. 'We can take it in turns to look at her through the night.'

At 2 a.m. everything was the same, tight vulva, no distress, and Amelia still massaging her friend's back. I went to bed and set the alarm for 4 a.m. It was a wonderfully warm night with the smell of new-mown hay flooding in through the open window. The moon was only a small crescent, too small to light up more than the cows' outlines by the gate to their field. I dozed, wondering how Brian could possibly sleep so deeply with his first grandcalf on the way....

Suddenly, I was wide awake. A noise? A moo? I shot across the room and shone the torch out of the window. Elizabeth was standing directly below our bedroom window looking up at me. She gave a very soft moo as though apologizing for disturbing me. I moved the torch to her tail and nearly fell out of the window with excitement – the water bag was hanging out! Forgetting to put on shoes, I ran out of the house, down the yard, over the gate and across the cows' field, arriving just in time to see a big fat calf nose dive into the long grass. It was the easiest and most perfect birth imaginable. I was just about to remove the membrane from the calf's head when, to my amazement, Amelia showed Elizabeth what needed to be done. Both cows rasped away at the calf, who must have wondered what sort of strange world it was where you got sandpapered before you were half a minute old.

I had no idea what the time was. The sun was just beginning to turn the sky pink, so I guessed it must be about four o'clock. Elizabeth and her midwife were making a good job of cleaning the calf, so I popped back to the tack room to fetch an iodine spray for the calf's navel. All yesterday's aches and pains had vanished. I could have planted a thousand chrysanths single-handed at that moment.

I sprayed the navel of Elizabeth's daughter, and helped her to her feet. She was enormous, the image of her Hereford father, with a white face, red and white body and thick muscular legs. She stood there for a moment, then lost her balance and fell flat on her face. 'Come on, you great lump,' I said, heaving her upright again, 'you've got to have some breakfast.'

She wouldn't have won any prizes in an IQ test, this huge baby. I took her to Elizabeth's udder and placed a teat in her mouth. She opened her mouth and let the teat fall out. I held her jaw open and squirted some colostrum down her throat. She swallowed it and opened her mouth for some more, like a young bird.

'This is ridiculous,' I told her, 'you're supposed to *suck*. Like this.' I sucked my finger, forgetting it was covered in iodine antiseptic. While I was spitting it out, Brian appeared in his dressing-gown. 'It's four o'clock,' he said, 'the alarm went off. Good God – what a *lot* of calf.'

'Hey, Brian – that's brilliant. We'll call her Lottie. She is a whopper, isn't she? I can hardly lift her.'

'You little beauty.' Brian squatted down beside Lottie and stroked her head. 'Has she taken a feed yet?'

'No, I can't get her to suck. Elizabeth's afterbirth hasn't come yet either.'

'It soon will once the calf sucks. I'll hold her head while you squirt some milk in.' He held Lottie's mouth shut round the teat and kept it shut while she swallowed. All at once the penny dropped and Lottie began to suck. Brian backed off carefully and shooed Amelia away in case her interference distracted the calf from this vital first feed. I gave Elizabeth half a bucket of fresh ivy leaves picked from the creeper growing up the walls of the house (ivy is a first-rate tonic for animals that have just given birth), and shortly afterwards the placenta came away with no trouble at all. Brian carried Lottie to a cleaner part of the field. Elizabeth followed anxiously, her eyes never leaving Lottie, while Amelia frisked around like a lamb, kicking up her heels at the sheer pleasure of being an auntie.

We stayed with them for a while and watched the sun rise and listened to the birds' dawn chorus. 'You couldn't have a nicer start to today, could you?' I said. 'Happy birthday.'

'Good Lord, so it is. Thanks for my present, Elizabeth, it's just what I wanted.' Elizabeth gave him a quick lick; he was no longer the centre of her universe.

After breakfast I suddenly remembered I hadn't put the afterbirth out of the dogs' reach. Brian's present-opening ceremony and phone calls to friends to tell them about Lottie had driven everything else out of our minds. Collecting some newspapers and an empty bucket I hurried out. I was too late.

'You *horrible* lot!' All five dogs scattered when they saw me, strings of mucus and membranes trailing out of their mouths. I chucked the bucket at them in fury, then tore back to the house to shut all the doors.

'Who are you shouting at?' Anne asked, putting her head round her kitchen door.

'The dogs. Bloody things have eaten the afterbirth. We *must* keep them out or they'll be sick all over the house.'

'Inky wouldn't eat afterbirth,' said Anne firmly. 'She likes her food cooked. You know how fussy she is.'

'If you let Inky in, you can keep her in your rooms today,' I said, 'and don't say I didn't warn you. I'm going to shut the others in a stable.'

Inky repaid Anne's trust in her by vomiting and having diarrhoea for the rest of the day. 'Can't understand it,' Anne kept saying, as the sawdust and shovel were brought into use for the umpteenth time, 'she's usually such a *choosy* dog.' The rest of the pack spent the whole of a lovely sunny day regretting their early morning feast, heaving and retching all over the straw in the stables. When we let them out in the evening, they slunk indoors, thinner and wiser dogs.

Within a few days, Elizabeth's milk, added to Amelia's, would have floated a battleship. Lottie suckled ad lib, but there was still 3 gallons a day for us. We sent out an urgent request through the SHA for another newborn calf, and while we were waiting for it to materialize, started to sell and swap cream. We could have made a pound of butter a day, but it seemed silly to go to all that bother when you could buy butter for 50 pence a pound and sell cream for £1 a pint.

The strawberry season was in full swing, so we began to swap cream for strawberries, keeping back enough to make gluttons of ourselves every evening. One of the nicest things about working hard physically is that you can eat pounds of strawberries with sugar and cream every single day without worrying about hips. Sometimes we sold the cream in Taunton market for 25 pence a quarter pint (less 12 per cent market commission), and although it was great fun filling the little tubs – like playing at shops – it took too much time driving to Taunton to make it really worth while.

One of my regular riding customers, a little girl of five, lived on a soft-fruit farm and her mother asked me if she could pay for Harriet's lessons in strawberries and raspberries. The ride should have been £2. Her mother always liked to buy a couple of pints of cream at the same time – another £2. Instead of money there would be boxes and boxes of luscious fruit, far more than £4 worth, so I began to give Harriet more time to repay her mother's generosity.

Brian didn't cotton on to what was happening for some weeks, but when he did, there was a big row.

'You've *eaten the profits*!' he ranted. 'Look, three weeks running where you should have written "£4", you've written "strawberries". I can't show that to the accountant.'

I haven't actually met an accountant socially, but I imagine they must be quite a strain. All that capital expenditure, overheads, depreciation, profit and loss. Did they, I wondered, *think* in accountants' language? Their poor wives...

'You're not listening, are you?' said Brian accusingly.

'Mm, of course I am,' I said, wrenching myself away from my imaginary accountant and what he'd say if his wife gave birth to triplets at the wrong end of the financial year. 'Strawberries you said. I've got to freeze them, not eat them. I will try, honestly. I haven't got much self-control over strawberries, have I?'

'It's a wonder you haven't got scarlet fever the amount you've been eating. How much does Harriet's mother charge per pound normally?'

'Ten or 12 pence I think. She gives me heaps more, though.'

'*Christ!*' Brian looked at me with something approaching admiration. 'And how many pounds have you frozen?'

'Twenty. Thirty maybe. I wish you'd stop going on. You and Anne have plenty too.'

'Even if Anne and I had 1lb a day each, it still leaves – strewth, I can't believe it. It leaves over 4 lb!'

'A week?'

'A day. Do you um, feel OK?'

'Fine, thank you. Did you know American Indians eat the whole strawberry plant? Roots, leaves, everything. They say it's the most powerful nerve tonic there is, and it stops you getting worms.'

'I don't think the accountant will be all that interested in Red Indians,' Brian said. He was obviously not going to be sidetracked. 'We can't afford to spend so much money on strawberries.' Overriding my argument that I wasn't spending money, he doggedly converted my greed into figures. What it boiled down to was that bartering was fine up to a point; bartering cream for strawberries was a very good idea, provided that most of the fruit was put down for the winter. What was not fine was eating £4 worth of strawberries a week, not unless I could find myself a rich husband.

He was in awe of my accomplishment, though, there was no doubt about it. He would be able to hold his head high when someone told him how their wife wove rhubarb leaves into raincoats, or knitted a new roof. 'Pooh, that's nothing,' he would say. 'My wife can eat a bucketful of strawberries in one go.'

The arrival of a new member of the family halved the cream ration overnight. Chocky was two days old, an Aberdeen Angus/Jersey cross with a coat the colour of Bournville chocolate. Elizabeth didn't really want to wet-nurse him, but was quite reasonable about it once she realized that he wasn't there to replace Lottie. Her milk yield must have been about 5 gallons a day, enough to feed both calves and leave a gallon for us. Chocky was not very bright; it took him over a week to recognize Elizabeth as his foster-mother. We would position Lottie on one side of the udder and Chocky on the opposite side so that they could each have two teats. Chocky seemed to think that Lottie's chin was the source of the milk, and would suck away at her face until we fastened him on to a teat. Amelia, in the adjacent milking stall, disapproved of all the merriment next door; one cow, one calf was the way things should be in her book. There wasn't much she could do about it, though, poor bossy Amelia with a nose quite out of joint now that Elizabeth had Lottie to look after. She was still boss-cow when it came to who went through a gateway first (cows are infuriatingly consistent over this particular piece of protocol), but over matters such as where-shall-we-lie-down-and-chew-the-cud-today, Elizabeth no longer deferred to her. We felt rather sorry for her and removed the hosepipe pieces from her Viking horns, but she abused the privilege – stabbed Brian in the shoulder – and had to have them put on again.

The long-range weather forecast was for a dry and sunny summer. This was perfect for the next item on the farming calendar – haymaking – but not so good for the newly planted seedlings. Brian and I had put in 500 cabbage plants one evening, five long rows in the same field as the chrysanths, watering them in from the stream, now a trickle, which ran down one side of the field. Within a few days over a hundred had wilted and there simply wasn't enough time or water to spare to revive them, so we left them to die.

The chrysanth seedlings were suffering from thirst too. None had died, but they weren't exactly flourishing; they just sat there in their orderly rows, looking exactly the same as when they went in. An old man, whose cottage bordered our field, kindly offered the use of his tap water one evening after he had watched us trying to siphon water from the stream. He was on the mains, he said, and we were welcome to give the poor things a drink to get them started.

Gratefully, we connected our hose to his outside tap and gave all the rows a thorough soaking. When we had finished, I took six pork chops round to the old man as a thank-you present and to my embarrassment he burst into tears and pushed the chops away. Couldn't touch chops, he wept, not since his wife died. He had come home from work one evening to find a nice hot dinner on the table and his wife dead on the floor, the tea cloth still in her hand. She had died transferring his plate from the stove to the table. 'It were chops,' he said, wiping his eyes with his handkerchief. 'I couldn't touch them arter that night.'

'I'm awfully sorry,' I said. 'I didn't know your wife had died. How long ago was it?'

'Twenty year come October. A good woman she were. Used to boil me pants she did.'

I gulped and said, 'Gosh, how nice, thinking, gosh how awful to be remembered as someone who boiled pants.

'Never had no use for bleach, she didn't. I don't mind bleach myself. Got to use something, haven't you?'

The question of *why* his underwear needed bleaching or boiling had not occurred to me. When it did, I couldn't wait to escape. 'I'm sorry about the chops,' I repeated. 'Perhaps you'd like some chrysanthemums when they bloom?' Fortunately chrysanths hadn't been his wife's favourite flower or anything like that and he said he wouldn't mind a few to brighten the place up. Thanking him again for the use of his tap, I left, still holding the chops.

The seedlings benefited enormously from the drink and sent up fresh growth quickly. They could have done with lots more regular watering, but the old man didn't offer any more and we didn't like to ask.

In any case, there was so much else going on that Brian didn't mind too much about the possibility of losing one crop. Horticulturally, his hopes were pinned on the anemones (not yet planted) and as always in June there was haymaking to think about and endless, *endless* weeding to be done.

He booked a contractor to cut the hay at half-term. As with any farming decision it was a bit of a gamble. Would the weather hold? Would we be able to get child (unpaid) labour? Would I be too busy with riding-school customers to help with the hay? Meanwhile, there was a village fête coming up, at which I had been booked to give pony rides, and a visit from Sara, whom we hadn't seen since Christmas.

She was in hospital having her tonsils out, and her visit would be more in the nature of a convalescence than an extra pair of hands. She could pick peas, we decided: the Kelvedon Wonder should be ready soon. And courgettes. (In the country courgettes do the most amazing thing – they turn into marrows overnight. You have to pick twice a day sometimes to stop this triffid-like tendency, something we had never had to do in London.) She could also collect the eggs, feed the poultry and see to the hatched chicks, all calm and restful jobs for a post-op patient. Perhaps some gentle hoeing too in the cool of the evening...

Sara, when she arrived, took one look at the list of jobs we had prepared for her and begged to be allowed to go back to hospital. It had been lovely in there, she said, colour TV, unrestricted visiting hours, noshy student doctors and a surgeon who told her that her mega-sized tonsils had made medical history and would be preserved for posterity in a glass jar.

'Go and sit in the garden and shell peas,' Anne said. 'You look dreadfully pale. I don't know what they've done to you in that place.' That place was London's newest teaching hospital, the recently completed Royal Free in Hampstead.

'I feel pale,' Sara croaked. 'I lost gallons of blood. They only let me out because I told them my parents had a farm in Devon.'

She rather fancied reading in a deck-chair under a shady tree with a few tins of Heinz baby food to keep her going, but no, her family had other ideas. Anne, who has a Christian Scientist attitude to illness – ignore it and it'll go away – wanted to see Sara bustling about in the sunshine; I wanted to pour sage tea and other herbal remedies down the aching throat, and Brian wanted her to lie in a darkened room all day listening to Radio 4.

A compromise was reached. She could spend the mornings resting, then lunch (call this *lunch*? Half a hedge put through the blender? Bloody hell...) then the calm, restful peashelling, etc. A few days passed like this, then one morning Gerry phoned. A reversed-charge call from a phone box in peak time could mean only one thing. Trouble.

Chapter Eleven

After setting up house with Gerry a year or so ago, Sara had got the nest-building urge. I half hoped this meant the start of the twelve boys I had ordered from our children (six batsmen, five bowlers and a keeper), but Sara settled for two springer spaniel puppies, Ruffin and Dylan. Gerry was keen on shooting and intended to train them to flush and retrieve, but, as yet, neither dog showed any talent for anything except hooliganism.

'It's Ruffin.' Gerry's voice crackled anxiously down the line. 'She's in hospital.'

'I think you mean vet's, don't you, Gerry?' I said. 'It was Sara who was in hospital.'

'Ruffin's in hospital now. I'm calling from London. Ruffin's in the animal hospital in Royal College Street. She's swallowed a whole jar of jam.'

'Oh, *Gerry*, you are a worry-guts. You didn't take her all the way to London just because of a bit of jam, did you?'

'You don't understand. She's eaten the jar!'

'Well, that's only 1 lb, isn't it? In fact, some of them only give you 12 ounces nowadays if you don't read the label...'

'The *jar*. She's eaten the *glass jar*. Crunched it all up. And the metal lid. Can I speak to Sara, please?'

'No, she's still in bed. There's no point in worrying her just yet. What did they say at the hospital? Are they going to operate?'

'Not until they've had her under observation for a while. She's got to be X-rayed to see where the lid is. The thing is, I've got Dylan with me – I've taken a couple of days off to be near Ruffin – and I've got nowhere to leave him during the day. Do you think I could send him down to you on the train? He keeps whining.'

'Yes, all right,' I said unenthusiastically. I knew something of Dylan's criminal record. 'Put him on the Paddington train and we'll collect him at Taunton.'

'Right, thanks. I'll phone later to let you have the train time. Oh, and Faith, there's one other thing. He might have swallowed some of the glass too. They don't think he has, but just to be on the safe side, could you give him cotton-wool sandwiches every couple of hours, please?'

I rang off and went to wake Sara. No more convalescence for her. She was upset to hear about Ruffin, but not at all surprised. Both dogs, being Welsh springers, stole for a pastime, and she and Gerry had tried everything to stop them, even filling a sausage with mustard and leaving it unguarded. 'We never even knew which one had taken the loaded sausage,' she said. 'They swallow things so quickly they don't taste them.'

'Poor Ruffin,' said Anne. 'She must have crunched it like a bone. She'll be all right, Sara, don't worry. You buy Baxter's jam, don't you?'

'What on earth does it matter what sort it is?' said Sara. 'I expect all glass tastes the same.'

'Ah, but it's not the same,' said Anne wisely. 'If you drop a cheap jamjar – a Co-op one, say – it goes into horrid splinters, but a good make breaks into chunkier pieces, like a windscreen. Not nearly so dangerous to swallow.'

Sara and I looked at her with respect. Anne, inveterate hoarder of every size and shape of jamjar, was an undisputed expert on the subject. She didn't know about lids, she admitted, but thought the plastic coated tin ones should go through without much difficulty.

Later in the morning I drove Sara into Taunton to meet Dylan's train. The guard, who had been looking after him, said he had been no trouble at all, and they had shared his, the guard's, elevenses at Reading. He was a remarkable man, a real St Francis. He said he had a large family of pets himself, all strays, at home. Always on the look-out for good homes for them, he hinted. Did a substitution job only yesterday. Didn't get caught.

'Substitution?' This sounded interesting.

'I switched a kitten.' He winked.

'Go on.'

A plain black kitten *en route* for Penzance by rail had escaped from its box in the guard's van and made its way along the train and into the first-class compartment. The sole occupant of the compartment, an elderly woman, took one look at the kitten, which was the double of her recently deceased Sooty, and begged the guard to let her keep it. As the guard knew where there was another plain black kitten in urgent need of a new home, he gave the woman Sooty's double, and the next day he substituted the other one and sent it on its way to Penzance. 'Twenty-four hours' delay's nothing for parcels,' he grinned, looking at his watch. 'I've got to go now. I hope the other spaniel gets better. Cheerio.'

'Bye. Thank you for looking after him.' The train pulled out of the station, leaving us with a picture of the guard distributing stray kittens like Maundy money to good homes all along the line.

Having Dylan as a house guest was rather like having an autistic child about the place. Ornaments, books, newspapers and table lamps all had to be put high out of his reach, the fridge door wedged shut with a brick and food double-wrapped in polythene to thwart that keen nose. A couple of days later, Gerry and Ruffin arrived. Ruffin had been unblocked by the excellent veterinary college, but had learned nothing from her experience. She fused the lights and nearly electrocuted herself on the very first evening by chewing through a live flex. Brian, groping round in the dark to find the fuse box, dropped a lighted match into a waste-paper basket. Blazing paper gives plenty of light, but is not a good thing in a house with a thatched roof, and my screams, added to Ruffin's, brought Anne out of her sitting-room. 'What's all this commotion?'

'Ruffin's fused the lights and nearly killed herself,' I said, hurling the waste-paper basket into the fireplace. 'Haven't yours gone off?'

'Oh, I wondered why it went dark. I thought a bulb had gone. Poor little Ruffin, she is having an unlucky time, isn't she? She'd better come and have a sleep on my settee. Come on, Ruffin, we'll listen to the rest of the play on the wireless, and you can have a biscuit.'

The next day, after several gentle hints from Brian along the lines of 'How much longer are you two going to stay?' Gerry, Sara and delinquent spaniels went home.

Home was a tied cottage in the grounds of a small estate in Sussex, where they were employed as caretakers-cum-groundsmen. Their employers – two families – used the place only at weekends, but expected the grounds, tennis court, swimming pool and garden to be kept in good order all the time. Sara and Gerry had a lot of freedom to run the estate as they thought fit, and on the whole, with help from plenty of mechanical aids, they made quite a good job of it.

One good thing and one bad thing resulted from their visit to us. The good was that they persuaded their employers to let them buy some ornamental sheep to enhance the Sussex scenery. 'Jacobs,' Sara told them firmly, 'are just what this place needs.' They were under the impression that Sara was a farmer's daughter and knew what she was talking about, so they placed an order with Brian for six Jacob sheep to be delivered at any time convenient to us. It was the most satisfactory transaction we have ever made. In one fell swoop, we were rid of over a quarter of our horrible leaping sheep at *Sussex* prices (which were double West Country prices) and, sweetest of all, made sure of sending all the ram lambs, as no mention of sex had been made on the order.

The gods don't allow you to have too much good luck at once: it unbalances their books. I was stripping Gerry's bed a few days after their visit, when suddenly I felt a violent sting in the tip of my forefinger. I tried to pull my hand away from what I assumed was a bee and another awful, hot pain shot up my hand and arm. My finger appeared to be trapped in the folds of a blanket. Gingerly I used my left hand to uncover the right and was aghast to find a fish hook embedded underneath the nail of my forefinger. It looked like an exhibit in a museum under none-too-clean glass and hurt like hell. Neve one to suffer in silence, I yelled the place down until Anne and Brian came running up the stairs.

'Gerry must have been tying his lines on the bed,' Brian said. 'Damn stupid thing to do. The nylon's got tangled in the wool of the blanket. I'll have to cut you free.' Anne fetched her dressmaking scissors and held my finger steady while Brian cut round the blanket leaving a small piece attached to the hook and line. They tried to pull the hook out, but the barb prevented it going backwards and my death rattles unnerved them. 'I'll take you to hospital,' Brian said. 'You'll need an anaesthetic.'

Sitting in the car with my hand on a cushion, I would have welcomed euthanasia on the bumpy drive. Brian decided to go to the doctor's surgery, as it was nearer than the hospital, but country lanes are not designed for passengers with fish hooks up their fingernails, and every gear change seemed to send the electrifying pain deeper.

'Dear me,' said the doctor a shortsighted, bumbling old man. 'Bless my soul, a fish hook. I've never seen a hook do that. Quite a problem, quite a problem.'

'Can you get it out?' said Brian, who had come into the surgery with me, and was hoping to be ordered out before the messy business started.

'Oh, yes, I can get it out. The problem is, it's in rather an awkward place. Probably the most awkward. You see, the fingertips are one of the most sensitive areas of the body and I've got to...oh, well, we'll see, we'll see.' He filled a syringe, held the needle up to the light and squirted a few drops upwards, just as we had been taught to do on the calf de-horning course. 'Hold the hand flat on the table,' he said to Brian, and to me, 'Grip the arm of the chair with your other hand, my dear, and try not to move.'

I had always thought that there were two advantages of living in the twentieth century – anaesthesia and *The Goon Show*. After having a sharp needle stuck into my fingertip, I have amended the list to *dental* anaesthesia and *The Goon Show*. We might be able to put men on the moon, but when it comes to fingers we are still in the Middle Ages.

Eventually, the hook was out, together with half a hand, judging by the yuck on the table.

'A number 18 hook,' said the doctor interestedly. 'I thought it looked like a 12 when it was under the nail. And this pink wool, were you using it as a lure?' Brian recovered surprisingly quickly from his ordeal as surgeon's mate, and soon he and the doctor were deep in fisherman's talk. Country GPs don't rush you out as town ones do, nor, it seemed, did they distinguish between the patient and the patient's chauffeur. Brian left with a list of good fishing places to try, and I, as an afterthought, got a finger dressing and a prescription for 'something to help when the numbness wears off'.

The something wasn't a lot of help, and to take my mind off my throbbing finger, I went off for a conducted tour of a pig AI centre that the SHA had laid on. We didn't have as many lectures and meetings in the summer as we did in winter, so when we did meet, it was non-stop shop-talk about each others' crops and animals.

Tactfully, the centre's guide broke into the hubbub of conversation and divided us into two groups before the tour began. In order to minimize the risk of infecting the valuable boars with our brought-in germs, everybody was asked to slip disposable polythene galoshes over their shoes before entering the main building. The group I was in started at the pig-housing unit, while the others went to the laboratories and operations room.

The boars' housing arrangements were superb. Each pig had its own bedroom (centrally heated in winter) and spacious dining area with sliding doors opening on to an enclosed, turfed garden. Thus he could choose how to spend his day – sleeping, eating or talking to his neighbours over the garden fence. It was like sheltered accommodation, with sex as a compulsory extra, and one of our group asked if he could put his name down on the waiting list. The boars themselves were in fine fettle, spotlessly clean and very friendly. The guide said the only problem they ever had was when their feet became overgrown due to lack of exercise. 'We can only let them use their exercise paddocks in dry weather,' he explained, 'otherwise the grass would become a mud patch.'

We saw their record cards and the feed stores where their

diets were carefully worked out according to their weights and breeds. Stud boars have to have a high-protein/low-carbohydrate intake in order to maintain a good fertility record. Twice a week each boar visited the ops room, the place where the semen was collected. The procedure itself was scarcely credible. In the absence of any female pigs, someone with a definite flair for getting into a pig's mind had devised some imaginative ways of catering for their needs. The semen was stored and distributed to customers on a sort of 'soup of the day' rota. If your Landrace sow happened to come on heat when Welsh or Large White was on duty, that was just bad luck and you would either have to wait until her cycle coincided with the boar of your choice, or breed a crossbred litter. Some pig-owners in remote districts had tried AI by post, but so far this had not been very successful. In England you can't rely on either the post or the weather – sperms don't like it hot – nor can you train a sow to 'peak' when she sees a GPO van coming up the drive.

On my return home, our own sows sniffed me all over. I think they thought I had been to the boar, which, of course, in a sense I had, and they were as jealous as anything. They made little oof oof noises, which is what they did to each other when one of them had been mated, and I had to have a complete change of clothing before they would leave me alone.

The hot weather held and conditions were perfect for hay-making. The contractor came one morning, just after the dew had evaporated, and cut 6 acres for us. The fields looked so smart with the tall grasses lying neatly in rows on the shaved pasture, and the smell was out of this world. Brian had his own hay-turning equipment, a machine called an acrobat, which fluffs the hay through the air, so he told the contractor that we would make (dry) the hay ourselves and leave it ready for baling in a few days' time.

Our fifteen-year-old nephew Tim came to stay at haymaking time. A nice lad was Tim, but so wrapped up in the difficult business of being fifteen that he was not a lot of help as a haymaker. He loved the *idea* of toiling in the hot sun with a pitchfork in his hand, but the reality of it – the blisters and the backache and the sweat – came as quite a shock. There was one field that had to be tossed by hand as it was too small for the tractor to turn round in. While Brian was 'acrobatting' the big field, Anne, Tim and I started tossing the hay in the small one. Within an hour, the first blisters appeared on our palms. 'A blister!' said Tim in consternation. Obviously, a blister was a new experience and one that rated a half-hour rest in the shade with his guitar. He composed very pretty tunes, rather Elgarish, but not much appreciated by the peasants while there was the best part of an acre still to toss and turn.

Brian finished machine-turning and joined us for a manual spell. Tim had by now started on 'Old Man River' and sang of 'body all-aching-and-racked-with-pain'.

'What's he on about?' Brian picked up a pitchfork. 'Come on, Tim, there are plenty of spare forks.'

'Tired o' livin' and scared o' dying',' Tim trilled on in his pleasant tenor. 'Hey, Brian, why do you keep your shirt on? It's beautiful to feel the air on your skin. Cosmic.'

'It's not cosmic, you work-shy young oaf. It's plain stupid. You'll get sunburn.'

Tim took a pitchfork and resumed tossing. He had never, he informed us dreamily, had such a lovely time. His blisters grew blisters. Cosmic. His body sweated. Another new experience. He would go to bed early and write a poem. By lunchtime, he was drunk on the smell of drying hay and sight of crimson poppies around the edge of the field. Brian envied him.

Two days later the hay was dry and ready for baling. It was a very fine crop indeed, composed of hard grasses, herbs, wild flowers and clover, which is how a permanent ley should be. (A temporary ley, or one that has been artificially pushed into quick growth by chemicals, gives you hay that is the equivalent of white bread – uniform, soft and not very nutritious.) The contractor reckoned there would be over 400 bales, which sent Brian and me into ecstasies, until we realized that each bale would have to be manhandled three times – once to load it, once to unload it and once to stack it.

'If you start baling down one side,' Brian said to the

contractor, 'I'll just finish rowing up that last bit at the top.' These were terribly nearly his last words ever. He swung himself into the tractor seat, reversed uphill and positioned the back of the tractor against the linkage of the acrobat. Leaving the tractor ticking over, he pulled on the handbrake before getting out to fix the link-pin.

'*Look out!*' The tractor, pushed by the weight of the acrobat, had started to move forward. Brian ran back to the driver's step and tugged hard on the handbrake. The cable had snapped. Half in, half out of the moving tractor, Brian had a fraction of a second in which to make a decision. If he got into the tractor, he would have to gain control before it reached too high a speed, and if he jumped out he ran the risk of being minced by the murderous prongs of the acrobat. Luckily, he belongs to that small group of men who have not the remotest interest in machines for their own sake (he once ruined a car wing by avoiding a frog in the road), so he abandoned ship, rolling well clear before the acrobat got him.

The tractor gathered speed and veered crazily down the steep field, dragging the acrobat in its wake. It must have been going like a bullet, for when it hit a ditch, it turned a complete somersault, sailed over a 15-foot hedge and crashed upside-down in the next field.

A cheer went up from some men who had been haymaking in an adjacent field. 'Go back and do it again,' one of them called. 'We couldn't see it properly from here.' They came in to look at the tractor which, incredibly, still had its engine running. 'Wonderful machines, these Fordson Majors,' someone said. 'They don't make them like that any more.'

'No, they make 'em with brakes now,' contributed another, and they all roared with laughter. To us the tractor looked a write-off, upside-down like a dead fly, but our knowledgeable neighbours said it would be as good as new with a few spares. Not so the acrobat, in pieces now, each piece embedded so deep in the bank that it looked as though someone had planted them.

The men returned to their own work and the contractor to his baler. Brian had livened up their day no end; it wasn't often you could dine out on tales of someone throwing a Fordson Major over a hedge. Oddly enough, nobody ever mentioned the possibility of what might have happened if Brian had not timed his jump right.

Humping the bales was huge fun at first, then not so much fun as the nylon baler twine bit into already sore hands. We thought we would have to cart all the bales in the Transit van, but a farmer neighbour wouldn't hear of it and lent Brian his second tractor for the whole afternoon. Tim found the whole thing 'way out', 'mind-blowing' – the way people (other people) pitched and stacked the sweet-smelling hay just like people had been doing for centuries.

It was extraordinarily uplifting to have a good hay crop under cover. No matter what the following winter might throw at us, there would be plenty of food for the livestock. And such food too. We knew it was good hay because a lot of it ended up in our bath water, giving us plenty of time to study it minutely. You could lie up to your chin in vegetable soup and count the different sorts of stems and seeds. Washing hayseeds out of our hair proved impossible until I had given us all convict haircuts with the kitchen scissors. We were amazed that Tim agreed to let me loose on his hair; I have a reputation for being a bit scissor-happy once I get going, but Tim said he didn't mind – it would be cosmic to donate part of himself to the compost heap and think of it nourishing next year's lettuces while he was doing his O-levels. His hair was beautiful – thick, black and curly – like a poodle's. He made me draw a boundary line with a felt-pen half-way up his neck and round his face to stop me cutting too much off. 'I don't mind the top short,' he said, 'but leave the back and sides long.' He sat on the garden seat holding a mirror and moaning with a kind of masochistic joy as the 4-inch lengths tumbled round his feet.

To everybody's surprise, not least my own, the finished effect was very nice. 'Who is this handsome stranger?' we teased him, and Tim, self-consciously touching his sculpted locks, put on a clean shirt and went for a walk in the stubble hayfield to get inspiration for a poem. It was going to be a forlorn/shorn type of poem, but when he actually saw the vigorous new growth of grass thrusting up through the stubble, he changed his mind and wrote a cheerful one instead.

The Jacob ewes were the next in line for a haircut. No kitchen-scissors job for them: their fleeces were too valuable. They had to be taken in the Transit van to a fellow smallholder's premises, where a number of us mini-flock owners had booked a shearer for the day. (Professional shearers prefer to do a lot at one place to save their travelling time.) Like many good ideas, it was fine in theory, but not so easy in practice.

We set aside the whole of the evening before shearing day to catch them. It was as well that we did because it took until after dark before the last one was under lock and key. Again, our farmer neighbours – the same ones who had witnessed the leap-frogging tractor act – were treated to free entertainment as we puffed and panted around the field after the jet-propelled ewes. Every time we thought we had them cornered, first one, then the rest, would see an escape route and leap free. I tried lassooing them, but the spectators' advice on lassooing made me laugh so much that my stomach hurt. I think the farmers would have helped if we had asked them, but we felt it was too feeble for words to be incapable of catching a mere six sheep. (Actually sheep, like children, are much easier to control *en masse*, but we didn't know it then.)

Ella, the expensive pedigree fool of a collie, watched the proceedings from a safe distance. She looked so elegant, silhouetted against the setting sun, but was about as much practical use as Tim's guitar. It was Ramrod and his love of his bottle that eventually did the trick. I fetched him from his favourite position by the kitchen door and led him to the sheeps' field. Cleo and Johnny trotted over to say hello to him, and so did some of the Jacob lambs; we still had all ten, as the six that were going to Sara and Gerry had not yet been weaned. Ella bounded down the field to play with her old friends and, in so doing, put herself between the ewes and their lambs. Quick as a flash I produced Ramrod's bottle which I had hidden up my jumper and ran back to the stable-yard. Ramrod followed his bottle, Cleo, Johnny and Ella followed

Ramrod, and the ewes charged at Ella. Brian herded the lambs behind and our farmer neighbours slumped over the gate and mopped their eyes.

Ramrod and I shot into an empty stable and comforted each other as all the rest of the sheep poured in after us. Cleo and Johnny had some sucks from the bottle as a reward for helping, then Brian carefully let the four of us out, while keeping the Jacobs in. 'Never again,' we vowed, as we staggered indoors for a cup of tea. We would sell them, eat them, *anything* but have to catch them again.

Next day Brian took the ewes to the shearer. (Lambs in their first year don't get shorn.) Everything went very smoothly for once. There were plenty of willing hands to help unload them into the shearing shed, and load them up again afterwards. The shearer charged £2 to do our six, and we sold the fleeces for £7 each. By law you are supposed to sell wool through the Wool Marketing Board, but not many smallholders do so. I can't remember the reason for so this ruling as I nodded off during the lecture on The Law and the Smallholder, but I think it's to do with not spreading germs through diseased fleeces. The only disease our sheep had was insanity, and as we were pretty certain that this wasn't contagious, we sold the wool to a local spinning club, which paid in cash and didn't demand forms in triplicate to settle the transaction.

Chapter Twelve

Those perishing ewes continued to be more trouble than all the other animals put together. We put them in the stubble hayfield to finish up the long bits round the perimeter, but they broke through a hedge and returned to their old grazing, which was intended for the still-grass-rationed ponies. Brian took precious hours off from gardening and repaired the hedges until they looked strong enough to withstand hippos. The sheep broke out in a different place. We advertised them in a local paper, but nobody buys freshly shorn, unpregnant sheep unless they can afford to wait a year for the next fleeces and lambs. They were too expensive to eat and in any case Tony had said the meat would be like shoelaces. So there was nothing for it but to keep them until they were in lamb again and hope they would not do too much damage in the meantime.

We sent the six ram lambs to Sara's employers, who were rich enough to afford 6-foot chain-link fencing. At the same time, we lent them Rocky the Shetland pony for their toddlers to ride under Sara's supervision. I wasn't getting enough small children to keep Rocky in work, and unless I took him out daily for an hour's lunging – tedious for both of us – he was going to get fat and bored.

Although happy enough to set off on this adventure, Rocky made sure he wasn't forgotten at home. One morning Sara phoned us from a police station some 6 miles from where they lived.

'Rocky's been arrested,' she said. 'The station sergeant wants to speak to you.' I longed passionately for a daughter who did needlework and married bank clerks.

Rocky had unbolted the gate to his field with his teeth and wandered the Sussex countryside, ending up on a dual carriage-way and stopping all the Brighton-bound traffic. Someone had telephoned the police and two officers in a panda car had parked on the central reservation, captured Rocky and taken him to the police station. Sara and Gerry, frantically phoning every authority they could think of, had been so relieved to hear he had been found they rushed out without any identifying documents. The station sergeant wanted me to vouch for them.

'Miss Sara Addis is your daughter I believe, madam? And the young man, Gerald Posner, is known to you?'

I said yes twice and agreed that I was the owner of a five-year-old black Shetland pony. 'I'm awfully sorry Rocky's caused you so much trouble,' I said. 'Please thank your two men who caught him, won't you?'

'No trouble, madam,' said the sergeant amiably. 'He came along very quietly – a model prisoner, ha ha.'

But even as he was being called a model prisoner, Rocky was adding to his criminal record. When Sara and Gerry left the sergeant's desk and stepped out into the police-station car park, they found that Rocky had untied his rope and had eaten every single geranium in the ornamental tubs round the yard. Crawling with embarrassment they went back to the sergeant, who was not quite so amiable when he learnt that his carefully nurtured geraniums had become Rocky's lunch.

Fortunately, all this was happening a nice, long way away, so Brian didn't feel duty-bound to go and re-plant the police tubs. He advised the kids about what varieties of geraniums to buy as replacements, then concentrated his energies on his own planting. The big day had arrived: he was going to plant 25,000 anemone corms.

The hand-propelled seeder, which had been tried out on our sitting-room carpet in winter, had to prove its worth in the soil now. Brian had carefully prepared the site, a south-facing sloping field, and pegged out guidelines for thirty-two rows. He filled the seeder's reservoir with corms and began.

'It's *working*!' I exclaimed. Even though it was brand new, I fully expected it to break in the first five minutes, as a lot of modern gadgets do. Of course, it was a very simple invention; there wasn't an internal combustion engine involved, so it had less to go wrong, but even so I was still impressed. There was a conveyor belt with corm-sized holes punched out at intervals (you got a selection of belts with the machine, each with different sized holes for different seeds) and as this passed through the seed reservoir, it allowed one corm to drop out every 6 inches.

Brian trundled the new toy along one of the pegged-out rows. Its red and blue paint gleamed in the sunshine, and Brian looked so pleased that I guessed he was feeling as bucked as I always do when I handle a brand-new pen and picture all the words queuing up to be let out. He stopped at the end of the row and parked the seeder neatly.

'What's up?' I called.

'Nothing. Let's dig a few up just to test it.'

Childishly we scrabbled in the earth, oohing in wonder as we found corm after corm nestling precisely 6 inches from its neighbour. The whole purpose in buying the seeder had been to save time and it struck us as a funny way of saving time if we were going to dig everything up to check it. Luckily, the novelty wore off after the first few dozen, so Brian started the second row, while I neatened up the excavations we had made with our hands. The seeder couldn't deliberately place the corms claw side down – it got about half right by chance – so I rearranged the misplaced ones. Brian said it didn't matter much as the corm itself knows which way is up and which is down; it has a built-in feeling called geotropism to help it find its way in the dark.

In no time at all the thirty-two rows were finished. 'Twenty-five thousand and no backache,' said Brian cheerfully. 'I think I'll sow some fodder beet next.' He changed the corm belt for a smaller one and wheeled away to the next prepared patch. The little beet seeds whizzed out of the seeder at 4-inch intervals.

'Just a minute,' I said. 'Fodder beet grows as big as footballs. Shouldn't you set the distance at 10- or 12-inch intervals?'

'No, that'll be all right. We shan't get full germination, you know. If it looks too crowded, we can thin out every other one and give the cows a treat.'

I didn't like the sound of 'we' can thin out. Brian has a

very convenient memory when it comes to weather. Here he was slum-sowing in June, feeling all hey nonny no with the sun on his back, but come the torrential rains later in the year and it would be a different story.

'I'm not kneeling in the mud thinning roots, thank you,' I said. 'Do set the gaps wider.'

'Seems such a waste of space. I'll compromise. How about 8 inches?' We have this conversation every year without fail, and every year the end result is what Brian calls a compromise. Sprout plants are set at 3 feet apart so that the picker gets soaked to the skin as gallons of water cascade off the adjacent plants; you have to hack your way through the intertwined jungle of sweetcorn before you can cut the cobs, and our French beans are a challenge to all but a trained ballet dancer. Without this 'compromise', our vegetables would be pickable only by helicopter.

With 20 acres to play in, Brian's horticultural abilities should have been fully stretched, but no. In true Gemini style, he wanted yet another string to his bow.

'I've reserved a secondhand polytunnel,' he announced one Friday. 'It was advertised in the local paper and the chap said he'd keep it for me. Do you want to come and see it tonight?'

'See it? Why can't we collect it?'

'It's 65 feet long. I'm not sure how they come to pieces, so I asked the owner to leave it standing so that we'd know how to put it together again.'

The tunnel proved to be great fun and affected our life more than we could have imagined. But dismantling and putting it up again was exhausting work. The tubular metal poles kept failing on our heads as we fumbled with unfamiliar construction techniques, but, at last, there it was – up.

If you have not had a 65-foot-long polytunnel of your own, you can't imagine what a wonderful thing it is. Step inside and you're in a new dimension, everything is suddenly calm and still, and the greenish light coming through the polythene skin gives you the feeling of being in an aquarium. Even the spiders aren't as scary as usual; they don't make those awful jerky movements like the ones in the bath do, and the other insects, protected from the elements, stroll around in such a relaxed fashion that you have plenty of time to watch them.

If I had seen little enough of Brian before the advent of the tunnel, now I was lucky to get a sighting at all, except for meals. He spent every spare moment in it, ostensibly making plans, but in reality just soaking up the heady pleasure of having a 65-foot blank canvas. Our friends used to joke that we could rent out the house for the summer and move into the tunnel. It got rather hot inside when the sun was overhead, but on a wet, cold day it was bliss, a small, warm world standing on a bed of rotted pig muck so fertile that you could plant a seed and practically watch it grow before your eyes.

We couldn't afford proper greenhouse staging – two 65-foot lengths would have bankrupted us – so Brian dug a channel down the middle and created two raised beds, shored in by planks on either side. It was too late in the year to raise tomatoes, peppers, melons and so forth from seed, so we played with a variety of perennials, house-plants and salads, learning by trial and error how to get the best out of a tunnel.

Being in an artificial world, the plants depend on the gardener for all their needs – water, light and food – and I think it is this responsibility that makes greenhouse gardening so interesting. An outside garden can be looked upon and, broadly speaking, treated as a whole, but in the tunnel every plant is an individual, with its own tiny territory and its own requirements. Some like to sit in the shade with a drink at their elbow, while others prefer to bask in hot sun all day and faint if they're exposed to draughts.

One small plant that Brian thought was a melon seedling turned out to be a pumpkin. He doesn't often make mistakes when he's transplanting, but in the green evening light the two species are almost identical.

'You can't grow pumpkins in here,' I objected. 'They'll take over the whole place. Can't you transplant it again outside?'

'I could, but it might be more interesting to leave it. I might get a hundred-pounder if it likes it in here.' He grows pumpkins every year and gives them to children's charities for Halloween night, or to me to cut up for the pigs. We don't

122

eat them. Some people do: they make jam, or that exceedingly nasty American mess known as pumpkin pie.

So Brian left the pumpkin seedling where it was, and it soon became apparent that it liked life in the tunnel a lot. It loved having its feet deep in manure and in no time had sent out powerful tendrils, shouldered aside its cucumber neighbours and worked its way purposefully right across the central path. Brian amputated its shoots regularly just to show it who was boss, and eventually, after producing a vast jungle of fleshy leaves, it stopped being so wildly energetic and settled down to parenthood. The baby pumpkins, marble-sized at first, became ping-pong balls, then tennis balls, and Brian started to use new words such as botrytis, mealy bug and canker.

Meanwhile, there was that other less tranquil life going on outside the tunnel; the one where you didn't say 'botrytis' when you saw unwelcome visitors arriving, but 'oh, hell' and worse.

'What are you oh helling about?' said Brian.

'Look who's driving in. Isn't it that boring couple who lived near us in London.'

'Oh, *hell*, it is. Let's be out.'

'Too late, they've seen us.'

'Hello, Hayseeds,' the man called out. 'We're touring the West Country. Couldn't go by without looking you up, could we?'

Brian and I exchanged covert glances, each accusing the other of failing to cover our tracks properly. We shook hands with them, and said hello to their three-year-old son who spat on Brian's shoes and announced that he hated Cliff Richard.

'He's tired,' said his mother, whose name we had both forgotten. 'We've been playing cassettes for him.'

'Come inside,' I said dutifully. 'We're just about to have tea.'

'Oh, don't do anything special for us, will you? Perhaps just a small Marmite sandwich for Crispin? I expect you're dying to know how we got Crispin, aren't you?'

I distinctly heard Brian say 'Chamber of Horrors?' but fortunately the parents didn't as they were busy trying to stop Crispin pulling Ella's fur out by the roots. 'That's enough, Crispy darling, the doggie doesn't like little boys.'

'She's fine with children, actually,' I said, 'and so is Parsley, but keep him away from Honey. If he pulls her about, she'll probably bite him.'

'Why don't you put your dogs outside if they're dangerous? I think Crispin might be allergic to animals; he can't wear wool, can he, Jack?'

Jack. I suddenly remembered who they were. Jack and Frances, who had a horribly tidy house and the sort of garden where the gladioli are manacled to stakes twice as thick as themselves. They had been childless then, but not for the want of trying. Frances had kept the whole neighbourhood up to date about her fertility tests, her ovulation charts, Jack's sperm count and other clinical details. The neighbourhood had responded with a big yawn. It wasn't that we were unsympathetic, it was just the constant repetition that made it such heavy going.

'Did you adopt him, Frances?' I asked, tipping cutlery on to the kitchen table.

'Oh, *no*,' she said, rather forcefully I thought. 'You know how we feel about adoption. We couldn't bring up a child not knowing anything about its background. No, we acted on the advice we were given at the clinic, and Crispin was conceived about a year later. They told us to put bricks under the bed.'

I stared at her. Was this the best that medical science in the twentieth century could offer? I had heard of corks in the bed for rheumatism, but *bricks*? Under the bed?

'You prop up the legs at the foot of the bed,' she went on. 'It helps to keep your body tilted at the right angle to retain seminal fluid after intercourse.'

'How interesting,' I said, trying not to catch Brian's eye. Frances had always been frank, but only in front of her female acquaintances as far as I could remember. Giving birth had evidently loosened her inhibitions. Crispin saved us the ordeal of further revelations: he started hurling forks at the cat.

'Stop it,' Brian said sharply, after it was apparent that neither Frances nor Jack was going to.

'Crispy, darling, that's not a very nice thing to do. Mummy's got to pick the forks up and wash them.'

124

'I hate that cat,' Crispin said, reaching for another fork.

Brian fetched a cushion and arranged Crispin's chair against the table. Crispin got hold of the sugar bowl. I decided on omelette as a quickish sort of meal and broke ten eggs into a basin. On Small's behalf, I added a whole spoonful of ground black pepper.

While the omelettes were cooking, Brian sliced some bread, Crispin massaged demerara into his hair, and Frances and Jack said how could we stand the boredom of the country after London.

'What about the doctors?' said Frances. 'How do you manage without a doctor out here in the sticks?' We told her there was a barber in Taunton who did a bit of blood-letting as a sideline and Frances shrieked with laughter. Crispin, not liking to be out of the limelight, painted the underside of the table with blackberry jam.

'Do start on the omelettes while they're hot,' I said, serving up the first two. Crispin's was on a plastic dish and he pushed it away angrily and made a grab for one on a china plate. Jack rescued it. 'Come on, old chap, you eat off the nice yellow dish and let Mummy have the nasty white one.'

'I hate red,' said Crispin.

'Is he colour-blind?' Brian asked.

'We don't think so. He calls all colours red, so it's hard to tell yet. Actually, I don't think he'd better have an omelette at all; he's allergic to eggs. He had a boiled egg recently and it made him go quite deaf.'

Brian said that if Crispin would try putting his food in his mouth instead of in his ears, it might help, but this logic didn't appeal to Frances. She had read an article in a women's magazine and knew all about allergies, so that was that.

During the sticky meal, the talk progressed from doctors to dentists. Frances had had her teeth capped by a dentist whom Brian and I had recommended after we had both been treated by him. He practised privately in Wimpole Street, and Frances said he had charged her only half his normal fee because she paid him in cash.

'Half price?' said Brian. 'You were jolly lucky, Frances. We paid him in cash too and he knocked off only about a quarter for us.'

'I think he needs the work,' said Frances. 'The overheads in Wimpole Street are colossal nowadays.'

'Mm, they must be,' I agreed. I remembered the dentist well, not his name, but, after six bridging and capping sessions, every detail of his face. He had dark brown eyes like a spaniel's, curly hair and a clear complexion. He had quite a temper too sometimes. Once, shortly after parking meters were installed in London, he left me in mid-drilling and strode across the surgery to the window. To my surprise, he wrenched the window up, stuck his head out and yelled, 'Piss off, you knock-kneed creep,' to a traffic warden who was sticking a ticket on his car. If he was still parking in Wimpole Street, his expenses by now must indeed be colossal.

After there was nothing left on the table for Crispin to mangle, Jack looked at his watch and said they had better be pushing off. No, they didn't want to look round the farm (thank goodness), they'd only looked in to see how we were getting on. Anne was coming in through the garden gate as we were going out, so Brian made the introductions. Crispin kicked earth in Inky's face and refused to say hello to Faith's mummy, so Faith's mummy wisely removed herself and her dogs indoors.

'Have they gone?' she said, emerging a few moments after Jack's car had disappeared.

'Yes, it's quite safe. Is Inky OK?'

'Her feelings are hurt,' Anne said. 'What a *ghastly* child. Have they been here long?'

'About an hour. Come and see the state of our kitchen.'

'Good heavens,' said Anne, when she saw the mess. 'You'll need to pressure-hose this lot. Who on earth were they – not smallholders, surely?'

'We knew them slightly in London. She was the one who was always going on about fertility tests.'

'I think I know who you mean. Gosh, fancy getting a horror like that after going to so much trouble. They should have had a dog.'

'Can I be excused kitchen fatigues, please?' said Brian. 'I

126

must go and shut the tunnel before the heat goes.' He went out, and Anne and I took damp cloths and started on the area where Crispin had been sitting.

'Isn't it a pity that such a nice-looking boy should be so badly behaved?' Anne said.

'Mm, nice-looking, wasn't he? Huge brown eyes and curly hair...' I tailed off and stared at the wall.

'What's the matter? Here, try bleach on that blackberry stain. Oh, look, it's *too* bad – the little monster's smeared it *under* the table; he should be in a strait-jacket.'

She carried on but I wasn't listening. I was recalling the rather wishy-washy blue of Jack's eyes. Frances had blue eyes too, highlighted with blue eyeshadow. So where had young master Crispin's brown eyes come from? And his temper?

Bricks under the bed, indeed. She'll be telling everyone next she got the bricks at half price too.

Chapter Thirteen

The riding school side of things was progressing nicely. The ponies had enough work to keep them fit and the money they earned paid for their shoes and for tack replacements, but not for their insurance. This was more or less how we had expected the riding business to run, quiet in term time and, with luck, busy in the holidays.

Each weekend was getting a little busier, with regular customers – all small girls – bringing their friends. On the whole, they were nice kids – the few exceptions, who sawed at the ponies' mouths because they had seen show-jumpers on TV doing it, got such a blistering telling-off from me that they didn't come again. My only regret was that my regular riders were all girls. I find groups of girls with that Celtic tendency they have to bear grudges for weeks, sometimes months, after an alleged slight has taken place, and their shredding to bits of absent friends, exhausting. Put a male in their midst and all this nonsense stops. If he's a big boy, they will want to flirt with him, and if he's tiny, they'll want to mother him; either way, they'll shut up about what the rotten old geography mistress said the week before last and concentrate on the new man.

So, until the school holidays began, I was stuck with my giggly girls on Saturdays and Sundays. They rigged up some brushwood jumps across the firebreaks in the woods and taught themselves to jump. My contribution to their riding education consisted of standing by the side of the track, textbook in hand, yelling encouragement or commiseration as the ponies either jumped or stopped.

All the ponies now wore rubber bits so that whatever mistakes I or my pupils might make, the ponies' precious mouths didn't get hurt. The ponies themselves were very pleased with the rubber bits, and shamelessly exploited their new freedom, swerving around the jumps when they had had enough. Shrieks of 'Monty, you *beast*, you were supposed to jump it!' echoed round the hills. The important thing was that everyone – ponies, children and I – enjoyed the rides, unlike some riding establishments, where the horses' happiness is scarcely considered. The girls soon learned not to depend on the reins for control, and I hoped this early training would stick and that they would never become heavy-handed.

One rider that I shan't forget in a hurry was my own mother. Anne's parachuting ambition had been abandoned when she read a newspaper report of a tragic parachuting accident. A young woman, making her first jump, had not been able to get her parachute to open and had been killed.

Naturally, Brian and I were shocked and sorry for the victim's family, but it was a relief to us that Anne had given up the idea of floating down into the orchard.

'I'm not going to waste my fitness training, though,' she said. 'I want to try riding next.'

'A horse?' I said weakly, knowing full well who was going to have to supervise this experiment.

'Of course a horse, what else – a motorbike?' (Five years later she did buy a motorbike, but that's a different story.) I'd like to ride Monty. He's the biggest, isn't he?'

'He isn't suitable for you to learn on,' I said firmly. 'He's a cob. He's too strong for you.'

'Too strong?' said Anne indignantly. 'I've seen small children riding Monty.'

'It's not a question of size. Monty's very well behaved with experienced riders, but he tends to take advantage of novices. You can start with Wellington.'

A few days later, when I had run out of excuses not to take her riding, I gave in and saddled Wellington for Anne and Noah for myself.

'What's that?' Anne, who appeared to be balanced precariously on Wellington's back, peered over his neck.

'A leading rein. I'll lead you from Noah.'

'I don't need to be led, thank you. I'll soon get the hang of it.'

I pretended not to hear and mounted Noah. 'Hold your reins like this,' I demonstrated, 'and keep your elbows by your sides. If you feel insecure, hold on to his neck – the strap, not the reins. OK?'

'All right, all right. I've seen you showing children all this. I won't hurt his mouth. What do I do next?'

'Push your heels down and keep your knees close to the saddle. Don't try to grip too hard, or your leg muscles will ache. Right, let's go.'

The ponies walked quietly out of the yard side by side. I was scared. Small children with their rubbery bones can take tumbles in their stride, but I didn't fancy seeing a pensioner – my own flesh and blood at that – nose dive off a 13.2 pony.

'He's awfully slow,' Anne complained.

'You're a *beginner*,' I snapped. 'You've got to go slowly at first. Aren't you even a little bit nervous?'

'I'm nervous that Wellington seems to have gone to sleep,' Anne said vigorously. 'Come on, Wellington, get a move on.' She urged him forward with her legs. Wellington quickened his stride and I hauled him back with the leading rein.

'I do wish you'd take that ridiculous rope off him,' said Anne. 'I feel such a fool being led at my age.'

We snarled at each other until we reached a bridlepath. Here I had to unclip the leading rein because the track was too narrow to ride two abreast. The path to the top of the hill was steep and Wellington lazy, so I was reasonably sure that it would be all right to let Anne go solo.

All went well until we reached the woodland rides at the top of the hill. Then Anne refused to go back on the leading rein.

'There's nobody here to see you,' I pleaded.

'I don't need to be slowed down. Stop *fussing*. Show me how to go fast.'

'No,' I said. 'You can't go fast today.' But I was wrong. She could and she did. How she got Wellington into a canter from a standstill I don't know. I do know that I aged twenty years in as many seconds. Noah and I raced in pursuit of my fast-disappearing parent. I knew for certain that she had never been on a horse in her life, so how on earth was she managing to stay in the saddle?

Wellington approached the row of brushwood jumps that my Saturday girls had put up. *Not* the jumps, I willed – *please* Wellie, not the jumps. Noah, my friend, my paragon of a pony, tore past Wellington and slewed round in front of the first jump. Wellington halted a few strides from take-off and Anne jerked forward, hitting her nose on his mane.

'Ooh, that hurts,' she said, rubbing her face. 'It's made my eyes water. Why did you stop so suddenly, you fool, Wellington?'

I clipped the leading rein back on to Wellington's bridle before pointing silently at the first jump.

'What are you pointing at?' Anne peered shortsightedly towards the distant horizon.

'These jumps,' I croaked. 'Right here in front of you. You could have been killed.'

'What jumps? Oh, are they jumps? They don't look very big. Are you always so jittery, Faith? You'd better give up this riding-school business if it makes you nervous.'

We went home the long route so that we could ride abreast all the way. I held tightly to the leading rein, and when I had got my voice back, tried to explain why it was not a good idea for beginners to canter towards jumps.

But it's so boring walking,' Anne protested. 'And quite uncomfortable really. I didn't know saddles were so hard.'

To my immense relief she had talked herself out of riding by the time we reached home. Not fast enough, she told Brian when he asked her how she had enjoyed it, and no, she didn't think she would want to try again.

'I think I'll buy a car instead,' she said. 'I'll treat myself to some driving lessons. I'll be able to nip into Taunton whenever I want to once I can drive.'

Brian and I looked at each other helplessly. Anne on a horse had been a heart-stopping experience, but Anne behind the wheel of a car? We could picture her like Toad, poop-pooping at all the other traffic (if she could see the other traffic – she was very shortsighted), urging her car to go ever faster.

'That'll be nice,' Brian said hollowly. 'Perhaps we could hire you out to Third World countries as a means of population control.'

'*Brian*,' Anne laughed. 'You really think I'm daft, don't you?'

'Of course he doesn't,' I said, before Brian could say yes. 'Only you're not too sure about things like left and right, are you? And you're too vain to wear your glasses outdoors.'

'That reminds me,' Anne said. 'My television's got lines again. Would one of you have a look at it for me, please?'

'Brian will,' I said. Although I was better than Brian at adjusting televisions (I was the one who gave the Granada man his tea and stayed to watch him work), I couldn't offer to do Anne's set for her because there was a large spider in her sitting-room: Gilbert, she called him. He was the latest of a long line of creatures who had found sanctuary under my mother's roof. He lived in a pile of logs in her inglenook fireplace and every night he came out and drank from a saucer of water she put down for him. He ate biscuit crumbs too, and, Anne claimed, watched the nine o'clock news with her while she had a cup of tea and the rest of the biscuit.

'Yes, I am a coward,' I said, anticipating her next remark, 'and if Gilbert puts one foot in our half of the house, I'm going to hoover him up. Are the lines on your screen going from side to side or up and down?'

'I'm not sure. I have the radio on for the afternoon play.' Brian looked at her blankly, then realized she was talking about cricket, another of her addictions. She would sit glued to the box, a veritable Wisden of knowledge when it came to test matches, and, like a lot of cricket fans, preferred the Radio 3 commentary to the TV one.

Brian fixed her horizontal hold and Anne was able to forget her disappointingly slow ride and direct her energies into abusing the square leg umpire at Lord's, who was not partisan enough to turn a blind eye when an England batsman was stumped.

The older generation are an amazing lot if our mothers are anything to go by. Shortly after Anne's hair-raising ride, Brian's mother, Addy, came to stay. She had had an adventure too, a first-time flight (in a jumbo jet, no less) and a month's holiday in America. She had stayed with her showbusiness nephew's family in Beverly Hills. California had impressed her, she said, with its scenery and beautiful trees and flowers, but she wouldn't like to live there. It was all right for Americans because they were used to it, but it wouldn't suit normal people.

'Oh, Mum,' Brian laughed. 'You can't generalize like that. What was abnormal about the Americans?'

'They're not exactly abnormal,' Addy admitted, 'but they are different. Bone lazy about walking for a start. Nobody walks anywhere. You never see anyone walking down the road or pushing a baby out in a pram – they all use cars, even for the shortest journey. I wanted to pop out for a fresh loaf – that was a joke, they wouldn't know a crusty loaf if they saw one – and when I said I wanted to walk, they looked at me as if I'd said I was going by broomstick.'

Brian conceded the point. 'OK, they're not keen on walking. What else?'

'They're wasteful. All that lovely sunshine in California, and, do you know, nobody ever hangs their washing out?'

'Where do they hang it, then?' I asked.

'They don't. They use tumble-dryers. Can you imagine anything more stupid than using electricity when the sun's blazing down all day long?'

On the whole, it seemed that the inhabitants of Beverly Hills had more money than sense. They paid people to cut their lawns, then spent more money in health establishments ridding themselves of the fat that they wouldn't have had if they did their own gardening in the first place. Logs were another source of amazement to Addy. Some people liked to have a wood fire in the evening to brighten the place up, but instead of buying logs, common or garden logs smelling of whatever tree they were cut from, they bought coloured, *scented* logs. These, Addy said, came in blue, green, pink and yellow and were impregnated with a synthetic scent so that the whole idea of a 'natural' wood fire was lost.

On the plus side, American shops were marvellous, much

better than ours. The assistants were well-spoken, clean and helpful, and the range of products, particularly in food shops, extensive. 'Their supermarkets put ours to shame,' Addy said. 'So clean. The staff keep bringing in fresh fruit and vegetables all through the day; beautifully wrapped it is, and much cheaper than over here.'

She had been taken to dine at Las Vegas. She couldn't remember who else was in the restaurant, except for Fred Astaire, who reminded her of the ticket collector at Paddington tube station. The Grand Ganyon had been very interesting, a bit big but lovely and colourful. The pot of tea that Addy had ordered in the Grand Canyon Café had not been at all colourful. 'Talk about too weak to come out of the pot! They'd made it with *one* tea bag. And that was on a string. I must say the waitress was very nice, though, she said they didn't have any tea leaves, but I could have another bag to make it stronger. It needed half a dozen extra bags, but I didn't like to ask because the poor girl had been on her feet all day.'

No, it had been a most enjoyable trip, but as far as Addy was concerned, it was good to be home; to be able to listen to *Woman's Hour* and *Afternoon Theatre* on the wireless instead of having to put up with round-the-clock television ('not even *good* television – it's all adverts') and to be left in peace to grow old saggily. Addy thought it pathetic the way the old folk in California fought against ageing. A keen gardener herself, she thought they ought to realize that when the season's over, the season's over and that's that.

Having both mothers minding the fort meant that Brian and I could get to some of the Smallholders' Association summer courses together instead of taking it in turns. We went on a conducted tour of a trout hatchery in Somerset first. This was a very popular event, as it took place on a boiling hot day, and there's nothing nicer on a hot day than to be near water.

We learned how a trout business is run, how the eggs are fertilized (a strange process, not unlike the goings-on at the pig AI centre), and how the young fish have to be moved from tank to tank as they grow towards the ultimate goal – the plate.

At one o'clock our guide left us to our picnic lunches and everyone kicked off their shoes and lounged on the banks of the reservoir to eat. As usual, we all talked at once, comparing calf weights, pig prices, hay crops and cabbage-root fly. A young dog called Doggerel was let out from his owner's car. 'I had to bring him,' she said apologetically, 'he eats the doormat if I leave him at home.' Doggerel was very well-behaved on the picnic, and daintily accepted cucumber sandwiches and lots of petting.

After the break there was a talk about the trouts' nutritional requirements and how to get the best conversion ratio so that the expensive pelleted feed wasn't wasted. It was apparent to us all that fish farming was a business with great potential if only – a collective SHA sigh – one had the capital to start.

The next outing was to a Cheddar cheese producer – it was too small to be called a factory and too streamlined for a farm – where we saw cheese made by traditional farmhouse methods using modern, stainless-steel equipment. Although the standard of hygiene was very high, it didn't prevent a few flies getting into the room where the curds and whey were separated. We saw how the whey was drained off, leaving the massive curds to be batted about in the tank by paddles until they were the right consistency for the pressing process. A few suicidal flies zoomed into the curds and got themselves incorporated into Cheddar, which was rather off-putting, until we realized that one fly dispersed in a 40-lb cheese was practically a homoeopathic dose and unlikely to cause trouble.

After pressing (a lengthy process that made me marvel at the people who had the patience to press and turn, press and turn for weeks), the huge round cheeses were wrapped in muslin and stored on airy wooden racks to mature. '*More* waiting?' someone muttered. 'Gosh, no wonder farmhouse Cheddar is so expensive.'

I was quite sorry that Brian had seen how cheese is made because it encouraged him to have a go at it himself. We had plenty of milk, and with Amelia due to calve in the autumn, he thought it would be a good idea to make a few practice Cheddars with Elizabeth's milk, and then do some really big ones with the milk lake from Amelia.

As he has even less patience than I have, it was hardly surprising that his cheese didn't work. To say it was a failure would be an understatement. It was a disaster. It stank the place out for a week, then it turned brown and rancid and was banished to an outhouse. 'It might improve when it's matured a bit,' said the ever-optimistic chef.

'*Matured*?' I choked. 'That cheese is *dead*, Brian. It's brown and wrinkled and crawling with weevils.'

'It's not perfect.' Brian was as reluctant as a mother with her firstborn to admit there might be a flaw in his cheese. But when a friend nicknamed the horrid object the neutron cheese (kills people but leaves buildings intact), he quietly put it on one of his compost heaps.

Chapter Fourteen

Way back in the olden days, when everybody could afford to go to the pictures, unaccompanied children who wanted to see an 'A' film used to hang about outside cinemas and beg kind-looking grown-ups to 'take us in, please'.

We were tickled to see a new version of this ploy taking place outside an amusement park-cum-children's zoo one day. We had taken the mums for a drive, and on the way home pulled up by the park to buy ice creams. Next to the ice-cream stall was the zoo entrance, with a notice saying Adults Free if Accompanied by Child, and next to the notice, but out of sight of the turnstiles, were three small boys touting for business. GET IN FREE CHOOSE ME said the handwritten cardboard sign safety-pinned to the jersey of one. Another offered ADMITUNCE FREE CHOOSE ME, while a third had bravely decided to state his terms with the simple but irresistible message: IM 5P.

I went over to talk to them while Brian queued for the ice creams. 'How's business, boys?'

'Not bad,' said the eldest cautiously. 'Do you want to go in?'

'No, thanks, we're just passing. Do you all charge 5 pence, or is he on special offer?'

'We don't really charge anything. People give us tips. Neville's trying out the 5p label for an experiment, aren't you Nev?'

Neville, who looked about six, nodded. 'I've been choosed four times today already,' he said proudly. 'How much have I earned, Pete?'

Pete, aged nine, drew Neville's wages out of his shorts pocket. 'Fifty-three pence. They always give him more than he asks because he's little,' he explained to me. 'One lady gave him all her change.'

'Tell me,' I said. 'Once you've taken your grown-up in, how do you get out of the park again without being seen?'

'There's a gap in the railings round the other side,' said Pete.

'Yeah,' said the third boy. 'Pete says if we get stopped from taking people in through the turnstile, we can take them round the back and charge them to go in through the railings. We'd have to change our labels, though.'

'I don't mind changing the labels,' said Pete. 'I could draw arrows to point the way. The ice-cream man will give us some more cardboard.' The ice-cream man, not surprisingly, was their friend. He kept a look-out for the man in the peaked cap, and let the boys take cover in his van until the coast was clear.

'Little devils,' Addy laughed as we drove away. 'Still, I suppose it keeps them out of mischief.'

Little devils like Pete and his mates were one thing. Real delinquents were quite another. John from Phyllishayes phoned up one day to see if we would be prepared to take a party of maladjusted children riding. 'There are ten of them,' he said, 'from the Midlands, and quite frankly the sooner they go back to the Midlands, the better.' He went on to say what a terrible time he and Lin were having with them and how one girl had already run away and had to be brought back by the police.

'Oh, John,' I said, 'why ever did you take a booking for maladjusteds?'

'We didn't know how awful they'd be,' he admitted. 'They've got three social workers with them, who are supposed to keep them occupied, but they don't – they let them run wild.'

Since we needed customers, just as John and Lin did, I agreed to take the children for a two-hour ride. With three other adults to help lead the ponies, I thought I could easily manage on my own, but when I met the social workers, I changed my mind and roped in Brian to act as the voice of authority. He was about to start making a pig-hut and was none too pleased to have to stop.

'They're going to be too much for me, Brian, really. I can't manage.'

'But if there are three staff to ten children what's the problem?'

'The staff aren't all there. They've got sort of far-away expressions and they smell funny. I can't explain. You'll have to come and see for yourself.'

We hurried back to the yard and found one of the social workers ('Call me Cy') and two of the bigger boys having a smoke about a step away from our hay bales. Brian plucked all three cigarettes from their mouths and ground them underfoot. 'Can't you *read*, you moron?' he snapped at Cy.

'What's the hassle, man?' Cy mumbled.

'Don't call me man. There are *three* No Smoking notices in this yard. Do you know what No Smoking means?'

'Ah, I get you. No need to get heavy. We didn't see the notices, did we, lads?'

The social workers, Cy, Len and Midge (we thought Midge was another man, until she removed her army combat jacket) protested half-heartedly as Brian made all the children turn their pockets out. Brian ignored them and put the collection of penknives, sheath knives, cigarettes and matches in the tack room. The children – six boys and four girls – kicked up clouds of dust and swore like navvies.

Before bringing the ponies out of their stables, I took the precaution of removing their reins. Hands that wielded knives were unlikely to be kind on ponies' mouths.

'Hold this leading rein, please,' I said to Midge. Brian and I helped the first five to mount and showed them how to hold on to their neck straps. Three of them could have been on painted fairground horses for all the interest they showed, and none realized that they were minus any reins. We demonstrated to Midge, Len and the mumbling Cy how to lead a pony from the left on a short rope. Brian and I took Jonathan and Noah, the two liveliest ponies, and brought up the rear with the rest of the children walking behind us.

'We'll go up the bridlepath to the top of that hill,' I called to Midge at the front. 'Then we'll stop in an hour's time and change the riders. OK?' Midge stared at her feet and said nothing. I couldn't see her face, but I guessed from the hunched

139

shoulders that two-hour walks were not one of her favourite pastimes. Cy and Len slouched along, apparently asleep, until they heard me ask my rider, a ferocious-looking black boy called Thomas, to tell me about himself and how he came to be maladjusted.

'You can't ask him that.' Len spoke through a tangle of unsuccessful beard. 'These kids have got problems. You're not qualified to handle them.'

'Shut up, you pretentious little twerp,' Brian said. 'If you're so qualified, why haven't you washed these poor kids or combed their hair? They stink.'

'Midge is supposed to handle hygiene,' said Len sulkily. He didn't like being called a pretentious little twerp, especially as two of the boys at the back were encouraging him to 'get' Brian.

'I'm not really maladjusted, miss,' Thomas confided to me once Len was out of earshot, 'but our mum's in hospital and Mary and me had to go into care for the time being. That's Mary up in front with Midge.'

'Is Mary maladjusted then?' I asked.

'No, neither of us. But our caseworker didn't know what to do with us while Mum's in hospital, so she thought we might as well have a country holiday with the bad kids. She's a nice lady our caseworker – she types.'

'How does that make her a nice lady, Thomas?'

'What I mean is, she's a nice lady anyway, but we know what she puts in our reports because she types them. You can't read ordinary writing upside-down, miss, didn't you know?'

Thomas, aged twelve, and his sister Mary, aged eleven, father unknown, mother in something (Thomas couldn't read very long words, typed or not), had weekly therapy sessions with the educational psychologist, known to all his young clients as 'the rapist' because that was what was written on his door. 'A right nutter he is, miss, honest, and his wife's a nutter too.' Quite how the psychologist and his compatible wife manifested their nuttiness was not revealed, but I did learn that he hand-wrote his reports. Bloody unfair, Thomas called it, not to know what the old git was saying about people.

I hoped the old git knew what he was doing sending two normal children away with savages, for the others were quite unbelievably vile. Hard-eyed and spiteful, they communicated with each other and with their staff in tedious whiny voices, every remark accompanied by the one inevitable adjective. Three of the boys on foot picked up sticks and began slashing at the honeysuckle and dog roses in the hedges, and when Brian took away their sticks and told them to stop, they threw stones at the ponies instead. Brian clouted all three of them very hard, which restored order for a while, but when it was their turn to ride, one of them took his revenge. Not on Brian, which would at least have been understandable, but on Noah.

At first I thought Noah had been stung by a horsefly, but when I looked I found that the boy had put a sharp flint between the saddle and Noah's back. The flint had pierced the skin, and blood was oozing out. To stop myself from making a few more maladjustments to the vicious child, I concentrated on calming Noah while Brian dealt with the boy.

'You'll walk,' he said, 'and you'll carry the saddle yourself. If you drop it, I'm going to put you head first in the manure heap.' A chorus of approving whistles and cat-calls broke out. The other children didn't give a damn about Noah, but they were all in favour of seeing someone – albeit one of themselves – ridiculed. They taunted the boy and dared him to drop the saddle. Either way, he was on a losing wicket and he knew it.

We walked briskly home, giving the party much less time than the two hours they had paid for, and not caring.

'Phew,' said Brian when they had driven away. 'Let me get to our nice sane pigs to cheer myself up.'

I agreed there was nothing like a pig to cheer a person up. 'I'll give you a hand with the new pig-house,' I said, 'hand you the nails and things.' Bramble and two of her sons, Hengist and Horsa, thought it would be interesting to help Brian too. However, pigs are not good at construction work, and after Brian had twice lost his claw-hammer, then seen a perfectly sound piece of timber crack as Bramble sat on it, he gave up.

'I'll make the house in sections over there,' he said, pointing to a level spot on the other side of the electric fence, 'then we can carry the pieces back in here and I'll assemble it while you distract them.'

He quickly knocked up a crude house – just three walls and a roof, while I had a stroll round the pigs' enclosure to see if any other houses needed repair. The five sows – Rose Hip, Briar, Bramble, Mimsy and Wimsy – were spending the summer kibbutz-style, each mother sharing the upbringing of their pooled piglets. Each had her own house, but once she had staked her claim on it by building a nest and giving birth, she lost interest in it and would usually prefer to move next door. The piglets hardly ever seemed to know who their own mother was, but would run happily from house to house, suckling from any of the five available milk bars. This cross-suckling is frowned upon in scientific circles, but we liked it. None of our pigs was ever ill or unhappy, and the piglets thrived by having a different-flavoured mum for every feed.

The houses, though, took a terrible hammering from all this coming and going. The sows used their front doorways as scratching posts, and the piglets, as soon as they had teeth, would gnaw away like beavers at the wooden cross-struts. Brian was constantly replacing sagging roofs or, as now, building a whole new house. We lifted the prefabricated walls over the fencing wire and placed them on some level grass next to Rose Hip's house. I held one of the sides and the back while Brian battened them together, then we raised the other side and fastened it to the back too. Leaving the U-shaped structure secured by 6-inch nails, we went to fetch the roof.

Where the myth arose that Gloucester Old Spot pigs are exceptionally intelligent I can't imagine. It was *not* intelligent for five sows to try to squeeze into a space no bigger than a large dining table, and it was not intelligent of them to stay around once they had demolished Brian's handiwork.

'I don't believe it,' he said, sitting down on some nettles and getting straight up again. The new house was now back in three sections. Like a barn-raising in reverse, it lay on the ground with the ends of the nails sticking up in the air.

'Quick,' I said. 'They'll hurt themselves on the nails.'

'Hurt themselves? I won't just *hurt* them. I'll kill the lot of them. Shoo! Shoo!' He waded into them, smacking noses and backs until they got the message and scattered. The piglets gazed wide-eyed like puppies, then bolted, their absurdly long ears flapping as they ran. We reassembled the house, nailed the roof on firmly, then stood back to see which sow would claim it. Disappointingly, none of them was keen on a house where prospective tenants got a smack on the nose just for looking round. 'I'll put a bale of straw in later,' I said. They'll soon go in when they're cold.'

The house stood empty for days, then suddenly it became a highly desirable residence, not, we realized, because of the excellence of the architecture, but because some of the hens started laying in the fresh straw. (Most pigs would sell their souls for a raw egg.) Interestingly, the pigs, who could and would kill a chicken if it stayed still long enough, didn't attempt to kill their egg providers. Maybe Gloucesters are intelligent after all.

'Fifty-four baby pheasants, last seen on the main holiday route to Minehead.' Addy, faithfully passing on a phone message, had a puzzled look on her face.

'Thanks, Mum,' said Brian. 'Do they want us to phone them back?'

'I haven't finished, Brian,' said Addy. 'The pheasants are lost – I understand that bit, you smallholders seem to lose things for a pastime – but what I can't believe is that they're apparently wearing *spectacles*.' She paused to see what effect this astonishing message would have. The look on her face, plus the conjured-up picture of fifty-four bespectacled pheasants on their way to a seaside holiday finished us.

'With suitcases?' Brian spluttered, 'buckets and spades? Oh, Mum, you should see your face.'

'*My* face? Doesn't it strike you as, shall we say, *unusual* for birds to be wearing spectacles? I thought it was a leg-pull, but the girl who left the message certainly wasn't in a joking mood. She sounded quite het up.'

She would be. Smallholders are so called because their scale of operation is small. A few animals, some carefully guarded crops, tiny paddocks where each blade of grass is cherished: fifty-four pheasants could well represent someone's entire bird flock.

For a short, experimental period after the SHA was founded, Brian and I acted as the association's SOS agents. In theory, anyone in trouble could phone our number and be put in touch with another member who had the appropriate qualifications to help. For instance, if someone's bees swarmed, we could tell them who had the experience, protective clothing and courage to go to their rescue; or if a member phoned up with an urgent request for cow colostrum, we could look down our list and tell them who was currently storing some in their freezer.

The system never worked. Since it depended on everybody always being available by phone, it couldn't work because people with holdings to see to are almost never indoors, except for meals. By the time the person needing help had got the message to us and we had given them some other numbers to ring, the emergency would over. A much better system evolved, born of necessity. Within the association, splinter groups geographically near to each other formed so that nobody had to rely on the phone.

'Pheasants, eh?' said Brian. Whoever had phoned was probably a new member, not aware that our Samaritan agency was a failure. 'Who do we know in the Minehead region who's good with birds?' Leaving me to explain to the bemused Addy that some pheasants do indeed wear spectacles, Brian began dialling.

Addy refused to believe what I told her about pheasant-rearing until I fetched a textbook and showed her photographs of young birds being fitted out with specs.

'Rose-coloured too,' she gasped. 'Well, I've heard everything now, I really have.'

'Birds can be quite aggressive,' I explained. 'But if they see the world through pink-tinted plastic, it calms them down.'

'I must show this book to Anne. I doubt she'll believe it either.' Tucking the poultry encyclopedia under her arm, Addy went to find Anne.

Brian finished his phone calls and came into the kitchen. 'I phoned a few members up north,' he said, and we laughed as we realized how parochial we were becoming, 'but the only one I could get was near Bridgwater. He's got a contact on a local radio station, so he's going to get a motoring flash put out, then go and help to catch them.'

'How did the pheasants escape?'

'Oh, the usual thing. He thought she had shut the pen and vice versa.'

'They might come back at feeding time, mightn't they?'

'I don't know. They'll probably panic when they get into traffic. Oh, damn, there's the phone again. We shouldn't have come in.'

'I'll go.' Sometimes prospective riding customers phoned during the day, even though I put 'evenings only' in my advert.

Anne, steaming with indignation about something, came in as I went out. 'Birds in *glasses* – it shouldn't be allowed...'

'Can't stop,' I said. 'Phone's ringing.'

'...haven't got the right *faces* for glasses,' she accused Brian, as if he were responsible. 'They haven't got ears, so how do they keep them on?' I kicked the door shut and picked up the phone. It was another SOS.

'I'm troutless,' wailed a youngish female voice. 'Bloody heron's had the lot.'

'Hello, Joyce' – Joyce was a newish member already getting a reputation for being a bit scatty – 'what's the trouble?'

'I *told* you. No trout.'

'Look, Joyce, I'm very busy. Can't you have a boiled egg?'

'Not for eating, silly, for filming. I've got TV people coming at three o'clock to film my new trout stream. [SHA members were often filmed or interviewed for the news media.] I took the netting off so that the viewers could see the fish, then I went indoors. Some damned heron has eaten them. Shall I phone the TV people and cancel? They can't film an empty pool.'

'No, I've got an idea,' I said, and with a guilty look towards the closed door – Brian's standards of integrity are much higher than mine – I told her what it was. Nobody but Joyce, I and a petshop assistant in Exeter would ever know what a rushed job it was to restock Joyce's pool with grey goldfish.

'...and what about worms, Brian?' Anne, the self-appointed champion of pheasants, was persisting. 'It must be most confusing for them to see everything in pink. They wouldn't know a juicy red worm from a slug, would they...?'

Quietly I slipped away and went to talk to our nice sane pigs.

Chapter Fifteen

Just before the schools broke up for the long summer holiday and life became a matter of twenty-five-hour days, Parsley and Elizabeth were mated to a dog and a test tube respectively. Elizabeth would have preferred a bull, but there wasn't a suitable one within reasonable travelling distance, so she had to make do with some Charolais semen and the AI man. She wasn't bothered; her life still revolved round her strapping daughter Lottie, a strong-willed tomboy when it came to things like having her face washed.

Parsley was mated to Nimbus, a young stud belonging to my new dog-breeder friend, Leoni. Nimbus was a very pretty dog, a near-perfect show cavalier, and Leoni was as certain as any breeder can be that his and Parsley's puppies would be a credit to us all. Breeding pedigree stock of any sort is fascinating – will the offspring have those most sought-after qualities of good physique and nice temperament? – and breeding puppies particularly so because you have to wait only sixty-three days to find out.

The nuptials completed, we turned our attention to the frenzied cycle of picking and freezing garden crops. Peas, two sorts of beans, courgettes and tomatoes passed through the kitchen at the speed of light *en route* to the freezer. New potatoes and salad vegetables we collected daily, eating what we needed and giving the rest to the pigs and the rabbits. All at once, after a spell of very hot weather, a sort of horticultural insanity swept over the farm. Every green thing suddenly seemed to be trying to outdo its neighbour in producing the biggest this or the most that. We measured a cucumber one day. It was 47 *inches long*.

'I don't think cucumbers are supposed to be this big, Brian,' Anne said, holding it up like a prize fish. 'Why don't you pick them every day to stop them getting out of hand?'

'I *am* picking them every day,' said Brian helplessly. 'It was hidden behind that pumpkin.'

The fact that 47 inches of anything could hide itself is an indication of the state of the crops in the polytunnel. 'That Pumpkin', now a standing joke among our friends, had become a botanical King Kong, and its infant pumpkins were already bigger than footballs and gaining weight by the hour.

Addy had gone home for a couple of months to see to her own garden. She would return in the autumn to help with the flower crop, but meanwhile we were three-handed when we could have done with six.

Once August was really into its stride, I was kept busy for a large part of every day with riding customers. I longed for the time when the government would elect a gardener as Minister of Education, someone who would have the power to change the longest school holiday to any other time than harvest weeks. But with our income being so frighteningly low (it didn't frighten us because we were used to it, but it grieved the bank manager to be forever dipping into the red inkpot), I had to take people riding more or less on demand and leave the others to battle with the crops.

I enjoyed taking the rides. My customers were mainly children of all ages and abilities, and occasionally a few light-weight mothers. Mrs Lacey, mother of the disappointingly conventional Tamsin, was a regular, and I looked forward each fortnight to a fresh instalment of the Tamsin/Mark saga.

The engaged young couple had reached the stage where Mark's parents had chosen and paid a deposit on a bungalow for them. Mrs Lacey, still at her wits' end to understand how she could have produced a bungaloid daughter ('She even let him block up the bloody *fireplaces*. Can you imagine…?'), had taken Tamsin on a shopping spree to Exeter to choose curtain material.

'She started off by looking at beige!' We were riding through the woods on Monty and Wellie when Mrs Lacey spat out this latest blow. '*Beige*. At their age! I said, "Tamsin, you've got beige carpets and beige wallpaper. If you don't get some colour into the bloody house, it'll be like living in a cardboard box." Do you know what she said?'

'What?'

'She said neutral colours were soothing. *Soothing*! What the hell does she want to be soothed for? They had some gorgeous fabrics in Debenham's, poppy prints and sunflowers and things, but Madam wouldn't look at them.'

'What did she choose in the end?'

'Nothing. We had a flaming row in Marks and Spencer, then a cup of tea, then we went home. She let me buy her a red cover for her toaster – big deal. Why should anyone want to cover up a toaster?'

Oh, come on,' I laughed. 'If you haven't got storage space, those pretty covers for toasters and food-mixers are a good idea. They look nice and they keep the dust out.'

'Dust? There won't be any bloody dust in "Mon Repos". No fires, drip-dry fabrics, any book that creeps in will be embalmed behind glass…' She looked gloomily into the distance.

'Are they really calling it "Mon Repos"?'

'No. They'll probably think up something just as bad, but at the moment it's plain number 29. Let's hope it stays that way.'

'Tamark,' said Mrs Lacey a fortnight later. 'They've called it Tamark. I ask you…like thermal bloody underwear.' She was more than usually strung up, and urged Wellington into a trot as soon as we were out of the yard.

'You're in a hurry today.'

'Sorry.' She slowed to a walk. 'I want to go further afield today, if it's OK by you. Somewhere without people.'

Since we seldom saw anyone except the occasional tractor-driver in a distant field, I thought this was rather odd. Even odder was her next remark: 'I say, er, have you ever smoked pot?'

'No, I'm afraid I haven't. Why, do you want some?'

She looked around to see if anyone had bugged the Forestry Commission trees: 'I've *got* some. I want to stop in the woods and try it. Do you mind?'

'Not at all. I've never done anything illegal before. It'll be what my nephew would call a New Experience.'

'I can't experiment at home,' she confided. 'My husband wouldn't approve, and I don't want to start a row with him.' I agreed that when you're at loggerheads with your daughter, the last thing you want is to open a second front with a husband.

We rode with unaccustomed speed deep into the woods, stopped at a clearing and dismounted. 'You hold the ponies,' Mrs Lacey instructed, 'and I'll get the bits and pieces together.'

'What bits and pieces? I thought pot was a cigarette.'

'It is. It doesn't come ready-made, though. You have to mix things together.' She knelt on the leaf mould under a tree and took out a packet of ordinary cigarettes, some paper and a small block of what looked like rubber. With some difficulty, she assembled two loosely rolled cigarettes and regarded them critically. 'I think that's right. A friend's son told me how to do it, but he didn't have time to show me. Have you got a match?'

'No.'

'Oh, that rather puts paid to it, then. I'm afraid I forgot all about matches.'

'No, wait.' I was not going to be rehabilitated before I had even started. 'Let's ride back, get some matches and come out again. We don't have to come all the way back here.'

The astonished ponies found themselves carrying us back down the hill at a canter and into the yard at a trot. There was no sign of Brian or Anne, which saved us having to invent a reason for collecting a box of matches and going out again. It must be awfully difficult being a full-time criminal.

We were glad to get back into the cool woods again. All that dashing about had made us hot and sweaty, and clouds of flies buzzed round the ponies' heads.

'It had better be worth it,' I said, sliding off Monty and loosening his girths. 'Now, what do we do?'

'Light up and inhale deeply. I've made us one each; more hygienic, don't you think?'

We lit them and inhaled deeply. The result was that we were both immediately seized with violent spasms of coughing. Tears streamed down our faces, our throats burned and we had to let go of the ponies and support ourselves against the trunk of a tree.

'I think we must be doing it wrong,' I gasped. 'It's horrible.'

'Ooh, my *throat*. They're stronger than Gauloises, aren't they? Shall we have another go?'

We tried again with the same effect. The cigarettes glowed hotly, like incinerators, giving off clouds of spicy-smelling smoke.

'That's enough for me, thanks,' I said, handing her my New Experience.

'I don't want any more either,' she said. 'I'd sooner have a Silk Cut. I must admit I'm disillusioned, though, aren't you? I thought it was supposed to make you euphoric.'

'Hey, look,' I said suddenly. 'Look at Monty and Wellie, they're sniffing it.'

'Good heavens. How extraordinary.'

The ponies were craning their necks over the cigarettes, letting the smoke swirl up their faces.

'Oh, they're not inhaling it,' said Mrs Lacey disappointedly. 'They're only putting their heads in the smoke to keep the flies off.'

We threw away the cigarettes and the unused block of marijuana, being careful to cover everything with leaf mould in case a passing deer wanted a new experience. Pot, we agreed, was a swindle, and a very expensive way of buying fly repellent.

A different sort of criminal story came up when I was taking a group of children riding one day. There were four boys, all strangers to each other, and a little girl who was the sister of one of them. She was a beginner, so I led her and let the boys go in front where I could keep an eye on them. They were very pleasant children, well-spoken, well-mannered and considerate to the ponies. They asked if they could race each other when we reached the grassy tracks.

'Yes, you can,' I said, 'but I'm afraid it's not much of a contest on these ponies. Noah always wins.'

'Noah?' they said in surprise. 'But he's so small. How can he beat Monty?'

I explained that although Noah was only 12.2, he was the

herd boss, and anyone trying to outdo him in a race was liable to get a nipped bottom. Impossible, they said, what about racehorses?

'Thoroughbred horses aren't very intelligent,' I said. 'They're obedient, which is quite different. They tend to do whatever they've been trained to do, whereas native ponies think for themselves. Anyway, you don't have to take my word for it. Try a few races and you'll see what I mean.'

I held Jonathan with the small girl rider and watched the boys ride four races. They changed ponies after each race, but the winner, regardless of who was riding him, was always Noah followed by Wellington, Monty and Jinks in that order. The boys were fascinated by this example of herd behaviour and wanted to know more about how ponies decide on a pecking order in the first place.

At the risk of sounding potty, I told them about some of the things I had observed at first-hand since having the ponies, and other incidents that I had read about. When I told them I had once sold a pony for being too well-behaved, they clapped and cheered, and I realized I had gone too far. 'I'm talking about ponies,' I reminded them severely, 'not boys. Now off you go. Keep in front, please, while I show young Lucinda Prior-Palmer here how to do a rising trot.'

When we caught up with them, they were comparing the fathers' occupations, a popular topic with small boys who don't know each other very well. Three of them boasted about their chemist/teacher/architect daddies, but the fourth seemed reluctant to talk about his.

'What does your father do, Jason?' I asked, not wanting him to feel left out.

'He's in prison,' said Jason calmly.

'In *prison*?' The other boys nearly fell off their ponies with excitement. 'Is he a murderer? Did you go to the trial? Did he have his picture in the paper?'

'That's enough, boys,' I said. 'Don't pester Jason.'

'I don't mind telling you,' said Jason. 'Daddy was a company director and he embezzled company funds.'

'What's embezzled?'

'Stole, stupid. Go on, Jason.'

'Well, he got caught and sent to prison, and on his very first day some bad prisoners duffed him up. They cut him with razor blades and he bled and bled.'

'I say,' said the architect's son enviously, 'have you been inside the prison, Jason? Is it like *Porridge*? Do they lock you in?'

'I haven't been in there yet,' admitted Jason. 'Mummy and I visit him in the prison hospital, but it's no different from normal hospitals really.' He seemed extraordinarily composed for a child whose family life had been shattered. His poor mother, I thought, I must say something to her when we get back.

We filed home, the children still talking non-stop about prisons and asking Jason if he could get them his father's autograph to show their friends. The mothers' cars were already parked in the drive as we turned in. 'Sorry to keep you waiting,' I called. They didn't mind. Of course they didn't. At £2 an hour, a free twenty minutes extra was quite a bonus.

'Hello, love,' said Jason's mother. 'Did you have a good ride?'

'Smashing. We had races and I won one. Can I come again?'

I tactfully withdrew so that his mother could say no-we-can't-afford-it-now-that-your-father's-in-prison, and went round the other parents to collect their money. They all drove off and I returned to Jason and his mother.

'Thank you so much,' she said, handing me the £2. 'Jason would love to come again, but I'm afraid it'll have to wait until the next holiday. We're off home tomorrow. Still it's been a nice few days, hasn't it, Jason? We love the West Country.'

'I'm awfully sorry about your husband,' I said. 'It must be a terrible time for you.'

'Well, hardly *terrible*,' she laughed. 'A bit of a nuisance, but these things happen, don't they?'

'When does he come out?' I asked. (Jason had not known the length of the sentence.)

'I think he's having the stitches out on Wednesday, so I expect he'll be home by the end of the week. They don't keep them in longer than necessary nowadays.'

I stared at her. 'Home?' I said. 'Not back to prison?'

She looked at Jason and began to laugh. 'I'll kill him,' she said affectionately. 'What's he been saying this time?'

'He said his father was a company director sent to prison for embezzlement.'

'He's an under-manager at the Co-op actually. But he's also been an MI5 agent and a cross-Channel swimmer, hasn't he, Jason?' She gave him a hug.

'But what about being in hospital? Did he really get attacked?'

Apparently not, or his wife would not now be leaning over her car bonnet helpless with laughter. 'He's having his piles done,' she giggled. 'MI5 agents have to keep fit, you know.'

Chapter Sixteen

Due partly to being seen giving pony rides at village fêtes, I found, as the holiday season ended, that I had acquired a number of local children as riding customers. This was a mixed blessing. On the one hand, I needed the business, but on the other, I didn't want hordes of small girls forever hanging round the stables getting in the way. I hated having to keep saying no to their offers of help, but since most children's help is worse than useless, I had to. It became quite a problem, and I don't think I would ever have solved it satisfactorily if a girl called Sarah Birdsall had not appeared on the scene.

Sarah B – we knew five Sarahs, including our own, and had to distinguish between them somehow – was eleven, a quiet, intelligent child, who lived about ten minutes' bike-ride away. She used to come riding whenever she had saved up enough pocket money, which wasn't very often, and after her ride, instead of lounging over the gate sighing, 'I wish *I* had a pony,' as all the other girls seemed to do, she would disappear. At first I thought she had gone home, but then I realized that the tack room was not tidying itself or the ponies filling their own water bowls. Sarah, without being shown what needed doing, had simply used her loaf and done it.

Gradually, by stages, I managed to get rid of all other would-be helpers. 'I've got Sarah to help me, thank you,' I would say, and even if Sarah wasn't actually present, they would melt away, with only the occasional 'lucky thing' to show that they minded. School term started, and almost immediately I had a fresh problem. Noah began to put on too much weight.

Without regular exercise, he always has a weight problem, and this particular autumn I was too busy on the holding to be able to take him out every day. For his own good, poor Noah had to spend over twelve hours every weekday in his

155

stable. Then it occurred to me that Sarah, although so young, was really responsible enough to take Noah out for exercise on her own.

With her parents' permission, Sarah began to come round to us after school. An hour's ride kept Noah's figure under control and still left Sarah enough time to do her homework when she got home. And she was conscientious to a fault. Whatever the weather, there she would be, pedalling into the yard on the dot of 4.20 with her riding hat perched on the bike basket. Sometimes I would get Noah ready for her, but mostly she groomed and tacked him herself, only to report to us when she had returned from the ride and was going home. Noah loved her, a great compliment, because he had had a traumatic foalhood experience in a slaughterhouse and still mistrusts most people.

It looked as though Brian and I might possibly be winning a few rounds in the 'earn a living off a smallholding' game. The riding side was firmly under control now that there were so few holidaymakers, and Sarah was seeing to Noah; the garden crops had done well; the cattle, sheep, pigs, rabbits and poultry flourished, and there were several tons of good hay in store. Our net income was around £12 a week. Next on the agenda was the climax of the growing year – the cut flower crop.

On 10 September, which was a Sunday, Brian proudly bore the first anemone bud indoors. We put it in a jug of water at 10 a.m. and kept finding excuses to nip indoors throughout the day in order to be the first to tell the others what colour it was going to be. The weather was unseasonably warm, and by 4 p.m. the bud had broken into bloom.

'Red,' we told each other excitedly, as if nobody had ever seen a red anemone before. Actually, to say 'red' doesn't really convey what a vibrant red it was. The anemones were a new strain called St Piran, bred especially for size and outstandingly bright colours, and the first one was more the colour of a Paul Crampel geranium than the muted red of an ordinary anemone.

'I think there'll be enough for a small picking tomorrow,' Brian said, and Anne and I trustingly, like the oysters in 'The

156

Walrus and the Carpenter', made preparations for the treat in store. We filled a bucket with water, lined a cardboard tray with clean white paper and put a few elastic bands ready to secure the bunches.

In the morning we milked and fed early, made do with toast for breakfast and sallied forth to the anemone field carrying a tray to lay the anemones on. The sun was already hot and had driven the dew off the grass by ten o'clock.

'They forecast an Indian summer,' Anne said as we walked along the lane to our land on the other side of the road. 'It would be nice, wouldn't it? It always makes the winter less – *oh*!'

'*Strewth*!' I said.

Brian invited the gods to do some very strange things to him.

The reason for three relatively normal people to suddenly say 'Oh' and 'Strewth' and something unprintable was in front of us. Instead of rows of anemone buds there was a sea of anemone *flowers*, a most lovely display of huge, wonderful, fat blooms.

'I must go and get the camera,' I gasped. 'I've never seen anything like it.'

When I got back, Brian was on his hands and knees picking, picking, picking, and Anne was walking up and down the rows saying 'Oh, my' and 'What *colours*'. If St Piran had engaged a top advertising agency, it couldn't have done a better job than the three of us trying to describe the sight. Each individual bloom was bigger and brighter than I had imagined anemones could be, but massed together they were breathtaking.

'Is this what you call a small picking?' I called, photographing Brian's back view with the lines of colour going away into the distance.

He laughed. 'I underestimated the sunshine. I'd no idea they would open so quickly. When you've photographed them, do you think you could pick some?'

'If we do get the promised Indian summer,' I said, squatting down in the next row and starting to pick, 'does it mean they'll always open like this?'

157

'I suppose it does. I hadn't considered an autumn crop would be at risk. We'll just have to watch them and catch them in bud.'

'What do you mean "at risk", Brian?' asked Anne. 'What's wrong with them?'

'They won't be saleable unless they're in bud,' Brian explained. 'If I'd known they were going to break so quickly, I'd have picked last night.'

'Not saleable?' said Anne indignantly. 'Of course they're saleable. They're only a few hours old.'

Brian shook his head. After fifteen years in the floristry business, he knew only too well what a retailer would accept and reject. 'Not this lot, I'm afraid. We'll pick them and keep them ourselves to see how they do, but I want only buds in future.'

The three of us picked until there was no more colour showing in the rows. We had to make two wheelbarrow trips to get the flowers safely back to the house, then spend more time rummaging in cupboards for spare jugs and vases. The house looked like the Chelsea Flower Show once all the anemones were in water, but we had no time to stay and admire them. 'Back to the fields,' Brian said with a fanatical gleam in his eye. 'Buds next.'

Buds were much easier to pick than blooms, but the novelty wore off as soon as the first stabbing pains appeared. Our muscles were simply not used to all this kneeling, bending and squatting, and protested strongly. Then back to the house for bunching. The single bucket and cardboard tray looked a bit silly next to a trestle table heaped with what eventually amounted to 140 bunches (twelve to a bunch). It was nice easy work, bunching, or so we thought, until Brian saw that Anne and I were picking up twelve at random before slipping two elastic bands round the stems.

'Sorry, girls,' he said. 'You'll have to undo them. You need mixed colours in each bunch, at least two whites and three other colours. And try to graduate your stem lengths so that the heads are at different heights and all the stems together.'

We soon learned how to tell from the slit in the bud which

was which colour, but getting graduated stems to match took ages. It was still only Monday, less than twenty-four hours since the first sighting of the first bud, and here we were surrounded by them. It was another example of the way nature delivers the goods in the country, quickly, almost violently, as if the sunlight, muck-rich soil and pure air had gone to its head. In London we had always had a successful and, with hindsight, *predictable* garden. You put in, say, dahlia tubers, and in due course some nice tidy dahlias would appear, not too small and not too big – just right for a vaseful on the hall table. Here in the country the same tubers would throw up great butch plants, like a ladies' football team, much too hearty to confine in a vase, and needing policing rather than nurturing. It was very exhilarating, but all too soon it got out of hand.

The success of any business has to judged by how much money it makes. If it's a horticultural business, the success or failure is twofold: first you have to grow a saleable product, then you have to sell it. Our anemone crop was such a thumping botanical success that, paradoxically, it became a financial flop. In short, Brian had grown more than the local market could stand.

We didn't realize this at first. He took the 140 pioneer bunches to Taunton and sold them for $12^{1}/_{2}$ pence each to three separate florists. By Wednesday another batch of the little tyrants were demanding to be picked, and by Saturday yet another wave appeared.

'If only...' we moaned (failed businesses always fall back on 'if only'). 'If only we could switch the sun *off* for a week.'

For the Indian summer was with us, and opening up the anemones faster than we could pick them. Hour after hour we would kneel in the sun, endlessly picking. We tried bunching them *in situ* to save having to start a fresh cycle at home, but it never worked because you couldn't always get the right colour mix from one place, and the elastic bands kept getting lost in the foliage. Also, the hot sun on the back of our necks made us feel cross-eyed, and we needed to get indoors to recover.

Every Saturday there was a market in Taunton, which would

sell smallholders' produce on a commission basis. We used this as our main anemone outlet, delivering 300 bunches early each Saturday, and going back later to collect the money and any unsold flowers. In addition, Brian would do a couple of anemone rounds during the week to florists and greengrocers in two towns. No one shop took more than three dozen bunches because country housewives, even farmers's wives, their purses bulging with government subsidies, are amazingly mean when it comes to buying cut flowers. It was quite funny sometimes to hear them in the market on Saturdays: 'I had a bunch of they beautiful anemones last week,' they would say, 'still as good as new they be.' And off they would go in their Range Rovers, pleased as punch that they had resisted the temptation to spend another 12½ pence.

Brian wasn't too downcast about the commercial failure. He was very pleased indeed that the anemones had lived up to their breeders' promise. They had grown well and evenly ('even' and 'level' are poetic words to a grower), and were so disease resistant that an epidemic of rust that, according to a Min of Ag leaflet, was decimating some anemone crops in the West, had passed us by.

'I should have planted ten times as many corms,' he said. Anne and I looked at him mutinously, so he hastened to explain. 'The crop is too big and too small – '

'Small?' Anne and I chorused. We were getting gibbon-shaped again.

'Yes, small. By professional growers' standards, it's tiny. If I'd gone in for more corms, I'd have had enough flowers to send to Covent Garden. As it is, the transport costs for just a few boxes a week wouldn't be worth it. No, it falls between two stools – too small for wholesaling and too big for local shops.'

The hot sunshine continued and we feared for our sanity. The anemones *had* to be picked, whether for sale or not was immaterial. If we let them go to seed, the plants would stop making new flowers and any late autumn sales would be out of the question. They would, with regular picking, continue to crop until the first frosts. Friends found themselves staggering home with arms full of anemones cone-wrapped in damp newspaper. Any we couldn't give away or sell were left to wilt between the rows. Housework, washing and ironing (oh, lovely pile of ironing on a rainy day with *Woman's Hour* on in the background) became a nostalgic memory. Dogs' walks, letters to friends, piglets' playtime, crosswords, everything went by the board. The only place you could sit down without feeling guilty was in the lavatory or when milking the cow.

Later in September, Parsley had five puppies. It was strange the way she always gave birth to five – this was her third litter – almost as if she knew she was making it easier for me to work out their feeds later on. This time she produced two boys and three girls, the biggest of which weighed in at a rather alarming 11 ounces.

Leoni had asked me to phone her directly the puppies were born. As an experienced breeder she could tell what the puppies were going to be like provided she saw them before they were more then a few hours old. After this, apparently, they change shape and you can't estimate their potential until they are nearly eight weeks old. I was a little sceptical about this claim, but pleased to have her look them over anyway.

She came as soon as I phoned. The puppies were six hours old, wriggly, tadpole-shaped and to anyone but me and Parsley, I thought, indistinguishable.

'I say,' Leoni said, gratifyingly full of admiration. 'What a superb litter.' She squatted down next to Parsley's basket and rolled the little rubbery bodies round to face her.

'Parsley won't mind if you pick one up,' I said.

'No, I won't disturb them. There's your best pup.' She pointed at one of the bitches.

I consulted the birth record – I weigh and name each puppy at birth – and was surprised to find that Leoni had chosen one of the lighter pups. 'That's Teazel,' I said, 'first born, 8 ounces. What about Fatty, Leoni? She weighed 11 ounces.'

'Crikey, did she really? Poor old Parsley. Let me see now, mm, yes, a very nice bitch but not in Teazel's class.' She examined and predicted for the whole litter. Boy and Twiggy, the second and third to be born were, in her view, show quality. Patch, the fourth, had a patch of pigment on his tiny face the size of a match-head. 'Pet home for you, my lad,' said Leoni. 'Mind you,' she added, 'price-wise, Patch should make the grade. If it wasn't for that one mis-marking on his face, he'd be nearly as good as Teazel.'

How she could sit there foretelling their futures on so little data was beyond me. But she did, and in the months and years to come, I never knew her to be wrong. She had firm views on puppy management too, and one aspect in particular intrigued me. Leoni maintained that a dog's adult conformation depends not only on its breeding lines but also to a very large extent on the sort of exercise it takes during puppyhood. Cobby dogs – that is thickset, deep-chested, short-backed animals, such as cavaliers and cockers – will actually grow into 'weedy' dogs if they are permitted to run about too much while they're still growing.

I found it hard to believe that an animal genetically programmed to be cobby could have its growth pattern altered by external factors, but Leoni assured me that time and time again she had proved this to be the case.

'I've seen puppies ruined by so called "walks",' she said. 'The owners don't mean to be unkind, but they don't understand. A pup gets more than enough exercise in a house with a small garden. It doesn't need to go out at all until it's about nine months old. If you let them run about in parks and fields, they grow tall and leggy in no time.'

'But if your theory is right, Leoni, wouldn't it apply to humans too? Are you saying that all short people have been kept in playpens to start with?'

'Yes,' came the surprising reply. 'Broadly speaking, a person's actual *height* will be determined by its parents, but the long bones in the thigh are certainly more developed in active early-walking children than in the quiet types who don't mind being in a playpen.'

'Coo,' I said, frightfully impressed and dying to start measuring people's thigh bones. 'I'll start a survey, Leoni. I'll ask mothers of grown-up children how mobile the longlegged ones were at what age.'

'In your spare time, I suppose?' said Leoni with a grin.

'Spare time? Oh, I see what you mean – the anemones. They must slow down soon, surely? Perhaps some sodium chlorate at dead of night...'

'They are on the vigorous side, aren't they? And your *apples*. I've never seen such a crop.'

'Apples?' I said stupidly.

'Apples. Round things. There must be 4 or 5 tons out there. You'll have to pick them soon.'

I put my hands over my ears. 'More picking,' I moaned. 'Please talk about puppies and long bones; talk about *anything* – but not picking.'

Chapter Seventeen

Apples come in different sizes and varieties. They grow on trees, and once a year they fall off and get eaten by whoever is underneath at the time. Like most orchard-owning small-holders, we folded animals in ours, a mutually profitable arrange-ment – muck for shade and vice versa. Some of our friends kept well-behaved sheep in their orchards, but as our sheep were certifiably not well-behaved, we reserved the space for pigs and poultry.

'Marvellous stuff, pig muck,' Brian enthused. He shook a bough laden with red apples to see if any were ready and they fell off.

'Stop it,' I squawked. 'They'll get diarrhoea.'

'They've got diarrhoea already,' said Brian wiping his shoe on dock leaves. 'They must have been eating windfalls for some time.'

We stood back and took stock of the problem. The orchard, comprising mainly cider-apple trees, covered some 3 acres. It was bounded on three sides by stock-proof banks and hedges, with the fourth side secured by single-strand electric fencing run off the mains.

'I could move the fence back against the far end,' Brian said, 'and leave them a 15-foot strip for a couple of days while we pick the apples. What do you think?'

'I think you're suffering from a touch of the sun. If we move their fence back, we'd have to move their houses too, and after we'd done that, we'd be too tired to pick apples. Why don't we put them in the stables for a few days?'

Pigs don't like to be 'put' anywhere. They like to choose. Occasionally you can trick them into choosing where you want them to go by presenting them with two equally attractive alternatives, in the same way as you would offer a fractious child the choice of a bubble-bath or a bedtime story. It doesn't always work.

I laid an enticing trail of chocolate biscuits from the orchard to the stable-yard, while Brian disconnected the electric fence. The sows watched us intently, then held a quick committee meeting. Chocolate biscuits meant trouble, they decided, probably a ring through the nose, or that rude AI man again. No thanks.

A sitting-down pig is as immovable as a slab of granite, and a pig that is comfortably full of windfall apples isn't easily bribed. 'Get *up*,' we gasped, pushing and pulling. 'Look – lovely chocky biscuits over there.' For a while they told us what we could do with our lovely chocky biscuits, then curiosity got the better of them and they lumbered over to where the fence had been. Having been conditioned from a very early age to the fact that electric fences bite, they refused to cross the great divide, even though there was no wire to be seen.

'Come on, Rose Hip,' I called. 'Be a brave girl.' Brian pushed and I waved a biscuit in front of her, but Rose Hip was adamant. We tried each of the others in turn, but nobody wanted to be first across.

'Let's pick up a couple of piglets,' Brian suggested. 'They might get anxious and follow us if they think we're stealing them.' We picked up two piglets and waited. Far from getting anxious about their children leaving home, the sows gave the impression of actively helping them to pack their bags. They nosed the unchosen piglets towards us.

'They want us to take the lot, Brian. Got any more bright ideas?'

We decided to sit at the start of the biscuit trail and wait. Sure enough, lured by the smell of chocolate, the sows eventually braved the wire that wasn't there and came rooting through the grass in search of Bournville heaven. All went well, and they reached the stable-yard in an optimistic mood.

'That's funny,' I said. 'I left a line of biscuits going into each stable. They've gone.'

'Dogs?'

'No, I shut them in the kitchen. Oh, well, never mind.

Come on, pigs, in here.' The pigs followed me hopefully into one of the stables and I slipped out again before they realized it was a trap. 'Sorry about this, girls,' I said, and shut the lower door.

'*Ramrod!*' Brian roared from the next stable. Ramrod shot out guiltily, his face covered in chocolate. 'He'll have to go,' Brian grumbled. 'He's crapped in the trough I cleaned out for the piglets.'

'Buzz off, Ramrod,' I said when he came to me for comfort. 'You're a nuisance and we're busy.' Ramrod shot off up the yard towards the rabbit run. Hamish, now father of dozens, was cropping the long grass at the edge and looked up at his large friend to find out what the fuss was about.

We were always saying 'He'll have to go', but actually his conformation as a ram was too good to waste, and we intended to use him on the Jacob ewes when they came into season. Our contribution to posterity would be *not* to add to the numbers of pure-bred Jacobs, but to help them into extinction as fast as possible. After Ramrod had finished telling his troubles to Hamish, he trotted off to find Cleo, who was rather at a loose end ever since Johnny had gone to the great baking tray in the sky. ('Eat Johnny?' Anne had said in horror, so we had swapped Johnny for a friend's Haydn, whom we could eat without guilt.) We shut all the piglets in the second stable and hurried away before they started objecting.

Brian had arranged for a cider-apple dealer to call once the orchard was cleared for action. He turned out to be one of those 'characters' who are such fun to read about in Fred Archer-type books and so impossible to talk to in reality. The broad West Country accent was wonderful to listen to, and, given practice, anyone can become attuned to differences in speech patterns, so it wasn't the accent so much as his attitude that was baffling. He wanted apples. We had apples. Nothing could be simpler, but as a dealer, simplicity was the last thing he wanted. Just as painters like to paint and racing drivers like to drive, so dealers like to deal.

The apple man, having surveyed the orchard with many 'oi dunnos' and 'proper middlings', found himself all at sea when he realized that Brian was not going to play a haggling game. 'What do 'ee reckon, then?' he demanded, looking at the sky.

'You're the buyer,' said Brian firmly. 'How much will you pay for these apples?'

The apple man winced. It evidently hurt him to see the climax approaching before he had had a chance to display his professional skills. He scuffed the grass with his toe.

Brian looked at his watch. 'I've got to meet a train at Taunton in half an hour,' he said. 'My mother's coming to give us a hand, and I mustn't be late. Now, do you want these apples or not?'

'Your *mother*? said the apple man in astonishment. 'You goin' to let an old lady up they trees?'

'She's very fit,' Brian said airily. 'She'll soon have these 5 tons bagged and weighed.'

'Four ton,' said the dealer swiftly and rather pointlessly, since any apples he bought would be weighed on the premises. 'I'll take 'em, mister,' he paused for dramatic effect, then said sorrowfully: '£35 a ton. Can't say fairer'n that.'

'£35,' Brian repeated, greatly relieved to have got the price settled. By chance, he turned his back on the dealer as he said something to me about Addy's train, and the dealer, automatically registering the turned back as a familiar part of his business ritual, immediately upped his offer to £40.

Brian stood very still and said nothing.

'All right. £45 and that's my best offer,' said the dealer. If we hadn't had had a train to meet, the silly twerp might have gone on bidding against himself for hours. As it was, we were only too happy to be getting an extra £10 a ton, a very fair return we thought for a few seconds' silence.

Addy took one look at the state of our half of the house, and clutched the kitchen table for support. 'What *have* you been doing? No, silly question, I can see what you've been doing. I thought you were growing anemones to *sell*, Brian?'

'It's a bottleneck,' 'Brian said unnecessarily. Every surface was littered with vegetables and anemones, and the passage inside the back door was piled high with boxes and buckets containing more of the same.

Addy fingered the anemones. 'Aren't they a size? I'd like a bunch of these in my bedroom. Which room am I in?'

'The one next to ours,' I said. 'We've got more helpers coming for the weekend – Tim and Marcus and a friend of Marcus – and we thought they could all go in the ghost's room.'

Addy looked dubious. She didn't think volunteer helpers should be asked to share with a ghost. She and I waded into the work in the kitchen, bunching anemones and sorting vegetables into 'freezer', 'for sale' and 'for pigs' categories.

'It's a shame to see these go to waste,' Addy said. 'Couldn't you put a table out by the gate and sell them to the public?'

'Not really. There aren't enough people passing to make it worth the trouble. And the vegetables aren't wasted, you know, we save on pig nuts if the pigs eat other things.'

'What about tomatoes? Do they eat those?'

'They eat anything. Brian has been taking tomatoes, cucumbers and peppers to Taunton on Saturdays, but it's a bit like the anemones. We can't sell as much as we'd like to. So he brings the unsold stuff back for the pigs.'

'I suppose people grow their own around here?'

'No, that's the strange thing. Smallholders and people without much money have kitchen gardens, but the rest don't seem to bother. The galling part is seeing housewives buying frozen vegetables when there's so much fresh stuff to choose from. I've even seen farmers' wives with tinned carrots in their shopping baskets.'

'People like that need their heads testing,' said Addy, and went on to tell me what the Beverly Hills housewives wasted their money on. It made Taunton's dietary peculiarities seem quite tame by comparison.

By Friday, Brian had picked the anemone rows clean and dared them to show another flower before Monday. We wanted the whole weekend free to see to the apples. Addy, Anne and I coped similarly with the garden produce and cleared up part of the house so that the helpers wouldn't feel they were living in a manic greengrocer's. The apple dealer had faded from the scene, leaving us in direct contact with the cider factory, who delivered piles of empty sacks in mid-week and promised to collect the full ones the following week.

Tim arrived first, by train, welded to his guitar and in need of another haircut. Then Marcus arrived, scattering chickens as he drove to the yard on a borrowed Suzuki with a pretty blonde girl riding pillion.

'This is Lucy,' he said, and added proudly, 'she's got her own licence.'

'Hello, Lucy,' I said, and thought oh, heck, why didn't he tell us his friend was a girl? Now I would have to sort out separate sleeping arrangements. She wouldn't be keen on sleeping with a ghost...'Come and meet Brian and Tim. You can bring your case in later.' I left them to wander round the farm, while I went indoors to reorganize beds.

Anne was in her kitchen de-fleaing Norman, a hedgehog, on the back step.

'Marcus's friend is a girl,' I said.

'A girl? How nice. What's she like?'

'Fair-haired, pretty. Doing history at Nottingham. Where shall I put her?'

'Has Marcus told her about the ghost?'

'I don't know. I don't think we should put her in there, though.'

'No, it wouldn't do, would it? Put the double mattress on the floor in the book room for her and Marcus, and leave Tim in the ghost's room.'

'But I don't know if they're sleeping together,' I objected.

'Don't be ridiculous. Of course they're sleeping together, and if they're not, they can start now. It'll save on sheets.' Anne gathered up Norman's fleas in a piece of newspaper and dropped the bundle in her Aga. 'Off you go, Norm.' Norman sneezed and hurried away as if he was late for work.

Gathering the apple crop was one of the best times we ever had as smallholders. It was a team effort, with the youngsters being sent up the trees like monkeys and we elders directing them from below. They started in shorts and T-shirts, but their arms and legs got so scratched that they had to put on tracksuit bottoms and old football shirts with long sleeves.

They scrambled up the branches until they found a secure foothold, then, grasping a branch in each hand, they shook the trees as hard as they could. Down tumbled the apples, mound after mound of sweet-smelling red ones and smaller showers of a quite rare, old variety called Newton Wonder. These, which were orangy-yellow, we left for our own use later on. The cider factory had asked us to include as few eaters as possible, apparently because they altered the taste of the cider, but to our surprise they said they didn't mind pig muck in their product.

'It's all organic,' said Marcus cheerfully. 'It won't alter the pH.'

'pH being short for "phew", I take it,' said Lucy, looking carefully where she was walking. She was enjoying her working weekend. Being one of the lads was nothing new to her, she assured us; her own brothers had trained her well. The kids pelted each other with apples and shouted things such as 'ship ahoy!' when they reached the tops of the highest trees. As they finished shaking each one, we would move in with hessian sacks and start shovelling. Hessian is lovely stuff to work with, warm and hairy and smelling like washed dogs. When the sacks were bulging with ripening fruit, the smell was intoxicating.

It was heavy work bagging up the apples, and our anemone-shattered joints ached. By the end of the first day we had done only about a ton, or 2240 lb, as someone worked out. On the second day the kids helped with the bagging as well as the branch-shaking, and we managed 1½ tons, which bore out Brian's saying that one boy equals half a man but two boys equal nothing. They *seemed* to be working when they weren't chasing Lucy, and their refreshment breaks were no longer than ours.

'We've decided to stay on,' Marcus said magnanimously over Sunday lunch. 'You've got so much food here that you need us to eat it.' He had been a vegetarian for two years and appreciated the garden's output more than most. 'Lucy and I have a few days' holiday owing, and Tim can bunk off school for a bit longer, can't you, Tim?'

'Yes. Can I stay, Brian, please? We never do much work at the start of term.'

'You said that at the *end* of last term,' Brian pointed out. 'Your parents aren't exactly getting their money's worth, are they?'

'Oh, come on, Brian, be a sport,' said Tim. 'I'm being educated here, aren't I?'

'Educated? I thought man evolved by coming down out of trees.'

Tim thumped himself on the chest gorilla-style, and in grunt language indicated that he'd like to phone his parents. Egged on by Marcus and Lucy, he spun his mother a tall story about how indispensable he was as a farmer's boy. He must have sounded quite plausible, as he was given permission to stay on for another two days. He rang off and leapt round the room exultantly. 'I'll write a lyric,' he said. 'Apple blossom and blue skies and...and...oh, something *great*.'

Brian, with great self-control, forbore to tell him that even poets would have a job to sound convincing if they wrote about apple blossom in September. 'What's all this about lyrics?' he asked. 'Have you stopped writing poetry?'

'Mm. I'm into lyrics now. I'm going to write a hit song and make us all rich.'

'Could you do it before tea, Tim?' said Addy. 'Then we could go on a shopping spree tomorrow instead of bagging apples.'

Chapter Eighteen

Nobody was more relieved to see the last of the apple crop than the pigs. The adult sows had sulked continuously for the five days of their imprisonment in the stables, turning their backs on us when we tried to reason with them and tipping their water trough over every time we filled it. The piglets shrieked when they heard human footsteps in the yard, ear-splitting screams that had us tiptoeing past their pen, stooping low so that they wouldn't catch sight of us. (A recent Ministry of Agriculture survey of pig units showed that the decibel level of cross pigs is actually harmful to human eardrums.)

As soon as the lorry had driven away with the 4½ tons of cider apples, we flung open the stable doors and stood back. The piglets were first out, twenty-three of them, pelting round and round the yard squeaking with excitement and kicking up their fat little rumps as they ran. The sows followed, slowly at first in case it was another trap, then gathering speed as they scented the great outdoors. They trotted purposefully down the yard, teats flopping from side to side, and then in at the orchard gate.

There was a shallow stream running through the orchard, and here they stopped for a moment to slurp a quick mouthful of water before clambering up the opposite bank. 'Oof,' said the first one ('oof' in pig language means 'gosh it's a lovely world'), then they all started oooing as they galloped towards their familiar old huts under the trees. Brian waited until the last piglet had pranced its way into the orchard before re-erecting the electric fence.

We stayed and watched them for a while. Some of the sows dived inside their huts and went into their compulsive-housewife routine, pulling out the straw bedding to air in the sunshine, while others found a good back-scratch against a tree trunk an

172

irresistible treat. There were still a few apples on some of the trees, which shook loose and provided the back scratchers with a tasty and unexpected bonus. The piglets bombed in and out of the piles of fallen leaves and bickered over the odd windfall. It gave us enormous pleasure to see them back in their right surroundings; looking at them so contentedly rooting, it was hard to understand how people can bear to keep pigs in captivity.

'Better get on, I suppose,' I said, looking at my watch. 'I'll muck out the stables first, then I'll give you a hand with the anemones.'

'Right. It shouldn't take long. I think they're *slowing down*.' He said this quietly as if the anemones would hear him and go mad again.

But they were getting less prolific. The shortening days and slight drop in temperature were making them almost manageable. Addy loved the whole business; she couldn't do much picking because she had had an operation on her kneecap and bending was painful, but she was a dab hand at sorting and bunching. Brian and I would pick and barrow them to the house, and the two mums would get them ready for market.

The chrysanthemums flowered and proved to be the most easily picked crop imaginable. We could stand *upright* and pick – an unprecedented luxury that hardly seemed like work. Because of the dry start they had had as seedlings, only about half survived to the flowering stage, and this was no bad thing as we were actually able to sell every single cut stem. They grew in four different-coloured blocks – light pink, white, yellow and bronze – and, unlike the anemones, the flower heads were nice and slow to unfold. That meant we could leave all chrysanthemum picking for Fridays and sell the lot in Taunton on Saturdays.

All at once, the hectic pace of the past few months eased. The hay was in, the apples gone, riding lessons more or less confined to weekends and young Sarah B looking after Noah's slimming regime. The vegetable and salad crops were submitting to the ceaseless picking of four able-bodied adults, and even That Pumpkin and its mates had slowed down. Addy said she would stay another couple of weeks, but after onion-stringing – another job she loved – she would have to go home or her own garden would have got out of hand.

On the last day of her visit, the four of us went for a drive across the moors. We stopped at lots of high vantage points and photographed each other against all the lovely bronze autumn foliage in the valleys. We drank ice-cold water from peaty streams and generally behaved like carefree holidaymakers, even to the extent of having a Devon cream tea in a tea shoppe.

'You ought to go in for cream teas on the lawn, you know,' Addy said to me. 'You've got pints of cream already, and once Amelia calves, you won't know what to do with it.'

'No,' I said quickly, but with an awful premonition that it would come to pass. Addy's casual remarks sometimes have that effect. (She once handed me a damp cloth and asked me to stand on a table and clean a grubby mark off the ceiling, which of course I did. Four months later I found I had re-decorated an entire house single-handed without quite knowing how it had started.)

'We're going to buy a second calf for Amelia to rear,' Brian said. 'If she's feeding two, there'll be only a gallon or so for the house.'

'So there,' I said, hoping my guardian angel was listening. 'Positively no cream teas.' For the record, my guardian angel, whom I have always regarded as a disgrace to his trade, was off on his hols again and I did get lumbered with cream teas – but that's another story.

On the drive home, we stopped to watch what we thought was some playful behaviour between a couple of moorland ponies. A mare with a small foal at foot was making repeated darts at another pony, a yearling colt. After a while we realized that the colt was her own last year's foal, now grown so big it hardly seemed possible that he should still want to suckle her. Again and again she rushed at him with bared teeth but he kept coming back. At length, she cornered him against a stone wall and gave him a good hiding with her back legs. The final kick caught him in the ribs and knocked the breath out of him. He got the message and went. 'There,' said Brian with a satisfied sigh. 'That'll teach him to play his horrible records half the night.'

Elizabeth had had Lottie on Brian's birthday, and the custom seemed to be catching, for on Brian's sister's birthday, halfway through October, Amelia gave birth to her calf. A bull, unfortunately (Jersey beef is dismissed by butchers as worthless), and as you can't call a bull-calf Pamela, we called him Jones – her surname – or Jonesy for short. Like all pedigree Jerseys, he was an outstandingly pretty calf, more like a baby deer, with a biscuit-coloured coat darkening to nutmeg brown on his legs and face.

Amelia became impossible after Jonesy was born. Always a bossy-boots, she now tried to use her horns like a scythe, menacing anything and anyone who came between her and her precious son. Elizabeth wasn't allowed to look at him, much less touch him, which seemed rather unfair considering the way she had let Amelia share in Lottie's upbringing.

'How on earth are we going to get near enough to milk her?' I asked Brian. We had put the word round the SHA that we needed a suckler calf, but meantime she would have to be milked out by hand once Jonesy had had his fill.

'Tie her up, I suppose. I must say, I'm not looking forward to it.'

Forty-eight hours after the arrival of touch-him-at-your-peril Jonesy, Brian picked him up when Amelia's back was turned and ran with him into the milking parlour. Amelia roared and galloped in after them. Brian put the calf in the manger and as soon as Amelia's head went down to protect him, the tubular steel sow-tie clunked shut round her neck.

'Got you, you old fool,' said Brian, patting her neck. 'Leastways, I've got your head. Now for the other end.'

Amelia's other end, she made it plain, was reserved exclusively for Jonesy. No boy of hers was going to share his milk with a mere human, not as long as Amelia had hooves and a whiplash tail.

'Quite a problem,' Brian said half an hour later. We were

both covered with dung and bruises, and the bucket was empty. Jonesy slept contentedly in the straw, his stomach full of gold-top milk. The trouble was that he couldn't possibly drink enough to empty Amelia's udder.

'Let's bring the other calves in,' I suggested.

'OK. Not Lottie, though, or Elizabeth will have a fit. We'll borrow Chocky.'

Amelia's lack of co-operation over hand-milking was as nothing compared to the tantrum she threw when asked to suckle the four-month-old Chocky. 'She'll kill him if we don't tie her leg up,' I said, watching Amelia lashing out. 'She looks as if she's taking aim.'

Chocky had more sense than to put his face anywhere near Amelia's lightning hooves, and he backed away. Anne appeared in the doorway. 'There's a man on the phone for you, Brian.' She came in and stroked Amelia's neck. 'Why are you being so long milking?'

'Sorry, I can't come in for the moment,' Brian said. 'Could you get his number and say I'll phone him back? We're trying to get Chocky to take Amelia's surplus milk, but she hates him.'

'She's colour prejudiced, that's her trouble,' said Anne. 'Try blindfolding her.' She went back to the house.

Brian and I looked at each other open-mouthed. 'What a good idea,' I said, 'not the colour prejudice obviously, but the blindfold. It might fool her into thinking she's feeding Jonesy.'

Brian draped a sack over Amelia's horns and tucked the ends into her collar. I picked up Jonesy and put him in front of her hind feet then brought Chocky into the danger zone. It worked. Amelia, not daring to move in case she hurt Jonesy, stood still and Chocky had a second breakfast.

'I'm going in to change my clothes,' I said. 'Don't forget you've got a man to phone later.'

The man, providentially, was a dairy farmer with a two-day-old bull-calf for sale. He was a popular source of calves for SHA members as he loved his animals and would never subject any of them to the stress and cruelty of cattle markets. He sold to private buyers only, and even then you had to be recommended by a friend. Brian reserved the calf by phone, then we drove straight over to collect it.

The calf, already named Lucky, was a cross-bred Aberdeen Angus, black as pitch. At two days old, he had had eight feeds from his own mother and now, colostrum-immunized, he was ready for fostering. We told the farmer about Amelia being so pig-headed, and he laughed and said if Amelia was his, he would triple-suckle her and forget about hand-milking altogether.

Amelia's face when she first saw Lucky was a study. Her eyes widened and she wrinkled her nostrils disdainfully, as if she really was colour prejudiced. We had intended to suckle two calves on her and take the rest for the house, but the dairy farmer's idea of triple suckling was much more workable in the circumstances. We took the adaptable Chocky off Elizabeth and, using the same ploy as before, fed him, Lucky and Jonesy on Amelia. After a few days, she grudgingly accepted the two extra calves, and though she would never be voted foster-mother of the year, at least she stopped trying to murder them. Elizabeth, Lottie and Brian resumed their peaceful milking routine with the mellow voice of Alistair Cooke to help the flow.

A postcard from Marcus revealed a world so far removed from an English farm as to be practically on another planet. Having saved up most of his days off throughout the summer, he was now having a few weeks' holiday hitch-hiking around Morocco and Turkey. He was with a friend, a boy called Gavin, whom we had never met, but who sounded every bit as daft as Marcus.

'Moroccans are rather uncouth,' read the postcard. 'We have been robbed at knife-point. Gavin appealed to their better natures, but there were a lot of them and they hit him.'

A few days later an air letter came with a fuller and, we suspected, a watered-down version of the incident. Both boys had been carrying money when they entered bandit territory, but not when they left it. They wandered hither and thither until they found a policeman. 'Didn't want to know,' wrote Marcus indignantly (he had never been abroad before), 'and had the cheek to *search* us! We asked to see an inspector or someone higher up, but this oaf couldn't speak English. Also he was armed.' Mary Kingsley, reproving nineteenth-century African natives with her umbrella, couldn't have sounded crosser. Armed police were simply not cricket. 'So we're coming home,' concluded the letter.

'Gosh, that'll be a blow to the Moroccan tourist industry,' Brian laughed. Perhaps it was a bit callous of us to find anything to laugh about in the boys' predicament; if they had been robbed in Taunton, I dare say we would have sailed into battle on their behalf, but when your offspring is geographically so distant, it seems a bit silly to do an Amelia and start waving your horns. We had a five-minute token worry, then decided that since the boys had access to pen, paper and stamps, things couldn't be too bad.

Sara phoned the same day. She had had a letter from Marcus too. 'They're OK,' she said. 'They've sold their clothes to buy food.'

'Oh,' I said, wondering what sort of person would *want* Marcus's secondhand clothes. 'Why don't they go to the British Consul?'

Sara giggled and said she couldn't quite see the British Consul in Heavy Metal sweatshirts. 'How are the puppies and Brian and Anne?' she asked.

'Fine. All the pups are walking now.' I settled down for a cosy chat about the progress of Fatty, Boy, Twiggy, Patch and Teazel, but Brian kept coming in and out of the sitting-room pointedly looking at his watch. 'Sorry, Sara, I've got to go,' I said. 'Attila's cracking the whip.'

'Hey, don't ring off. I want to hear about your Clydesdales.'

'The course starts on Monday,' I said. 'I shan't be home until after dark, so ring as late as possible and I'll tell you all about it.'

I didn't really have Clydesdales, but I did have the chance to go on an Agricultural Training Board course of Heavy Horse Driving, an opportunity I wouldn't have missed for anything. Apart from anything else, it was free – the ATB paid the course fees and even the travelling expenses. The week-long course was held on the instructor's farm in Dorset some 50 miles away, a long drive to and fro each day. I was lucky enough to be able to go with a friend called Jayne in her car. Jayne farmed a suckler herd of Jerseys in Somerset and had to travel more or less past our place on the way to Dorset, so we were able to keep each other awake on the drive.

There were seven of us on the course, four residential students, strangers to us, with Jayne and myself, plus another SHA friend called Penny, attending daily. The instructor's name was Charlie, and the two four-year-old Clydesdales were called Peanuts and Popcorn.

Before the end of the first morning, we had been taught the names of all the bits and pieces that make up a cart-horse's wardrobe, the correct way to put it on the horse, then how to hitch a wagon to the tug chains. Peanuts and Popcorn were endlessly patient with us, lowering their heads to enable us to slip the huge collars on without having to stand on a box. 'They're only babies,' Charlie warned. 'Don't expect miracles from them.' He was training Peanuts and Popcorn at the same time as us, and making a good job of it, we all agreed over a packed lunch.

A draught-horse is directed mainly by voice. To go forwards the command is 'walk on' (the same as for a ridden horse) and backwards is 'back'. The right and left words vary from district to district in Britain, and we were taught to say 'get off' for right and 'come here' for left. Peanuts and Popcorn both spoke English, unlike some of Charlie's imported Ardennes horses, who spoke only French and had to have a crash language course before they could start work.

In the afternoon we all took turns at solo driving, standing on the wooden boards of a flat-bed wagon and guiding the 17-hand Clydesdales around an obstacle course. Their mouths were amazingly soft – a tribute to Charlie's gentle training and insistence on straight-bar snaffle bits – needing only the lightest touch on the reins to turn and halt them. All too soon, the light began to fade and it was time to put the massive babies back in their stables and head for home.

We progressed from single-horse driving to pairs. Peanuts

was inclined to let Popcorn do most of the pulling and Charlie had to show us how to push Peanuts into his collar (by voice only), while at the same time praising Popcorn for doing his work properly. It took a lot of practice to say 'Peanuts *walk on*' in a sharp voice, and then change to a soothing 'Good boy, Popcorn, stea–dy.'

The ground was too hard for plough work, so we chain-harrowed a field instead, going up and down in straight(ish) lines in a cloud of chalk dust. Our hardest test was to drive a cart with the horses in tandem into a smallish yard ('Mind the sodding *gatepost*,' shouted Charlie in the voice he usually reserved for Peanuts), then back them up to a barn door. Controlling eight legs and four wheels in reverse is not easy. Draught-horses with feet the size of dinner plates are simply not good at taking the little mincing steps that are necessary for this delicate manoeuvre, and even when one got it right, the other one had only to put in an extra stride and the cart would end up at 45 degrees instead of straight.

Never has a week passed so quickly. The combination of good company, good teaching, leather and horse smells, plus beautiful scenery – some of the beech woodland almost seemed to be on fire with autumn colours – was as bracing as a cold shower on a hot day. But suddenly it was the last day, time to attend a lecture on feet by a visiting vet, then to say goodbye. With a repertoire of new puns gleaned from harness parts ('Hames, sweet hames', 'Once more into the breeches' and so forth) we took leave of our fellow pupils, Charlie, and those lovable giants, Peanuts and Popcorn, the gentlest toe-crushers ever born.

Chapter Nineteen

'I'm so glad to have you at home again,' said Brian.

'Gosh, thanks,' I said, touched and surprised. 'Couldn't you find any female company while I was off the premises?'

'The cement-mixer's come. We can get on twice as fast now you're back.'

Oh, well, it's nice to be wanted for something. The cement-mixer, borrowed from a friend, was a hand-driven one and had a wheel with grips round it like a ship's wheel, which turned a drum containing the cement/sand/water mixture. It wasn't hard work, but it was boring churning the aggregate round and round until it was sloppy.

When a building course had been requested by SHA members, Brian had been quick to offer our premises as the teaching site. We had a convenient 15 x 10 gap at the end of one stable block, which was just the right size for ten people to work on at once within earshot of the instructor. We were taught by a qualified builder called Derek – one of our own members – who was an excellent teacher. Once a week everybody assembled on site and under Derek's guidance would learn one stage of the construction of a new stable. Then Brian would complete that part of the work during the rest of the week, and leave everything ready for Derek to show us how to do the next bit.

Because of being on the driving course, I had missed one building lesson, but I soon mugged it up from Brian's notes, skipping the grey areas that told you how to estimate for materials by measuring different planes.

Building wasn't all that difficult, we discovered. The secret of success lay in getting the first stages 100 per cent right. The ground has to be levelled, damp-proofed – polythene feed sacks for this – then boxed in with heavy planks of wood. We all became familiar with terms such as 'shuttering' and 'raising the fat', and didn't dare move a step without the ever-present 'bubble' (spirit level).

As the weeks went by, the stable grew most satisfactorily. Everyone helped to lay a cement floor which sloped into an outlet pipe, then, when that was dry, we all made breeze-block walls, leaving gaps for a window and a door. You had to check the level of each brick course before laying the next in case it had bumps in, and we soon learned to get it right the first time to save the horrible messy job of removing some of the sandwiching layer of cement. Everybody complained about sore hands and aching backs, but nobody dropped out. Six weeks after the first weed had been pulled to start clearing the site, a smart new stable existed – a stable with a small mystery about it.

In years to come architectural historians are going to have a job to puzzle out how a West Country outbuilding came to have a door with a smart London manufacturer's stamp on it. What happened was that in 1977 London's Alexandra Palace racecourse was closed down and a demolition firm moved in. Sara and Gerry were living in London at the time and thought it such a dreadful waste to see craftsman-built stuff being bonfired that they rescued six stable doors. It was a real labour of love; they had no transport and each half of each oak door weighed 70 lb. They struggled to and fro twelve times on foot, storing the doors in a friend's garden, then Brian took the Transit to London and collected them.

We had already used one to replace a rotting 200-year-old door on a barn and, oddly enough, it didn't look a bit out of place. Even on the new stable, which itself seemed slightly self-conscious before the walls weathered, the second racecourse door was just the job; seasoned oak was evidently good at bringing Tudor and modern styles together.

Another course, more academic, was the eagerly awaited horticultural one. This was laid on by the Extramural Department of Bristol University, the same body that had given us the animal husbandry course last autumn. Again the classroom was packed, and again the calibre of the lecturers was such that even statistics about soil microbes was put across so interestingly that you could practically hear the little microbes chomping away at their nitrogen at so much a square yard.

The Smallholders' Association was now in its second year, and I think it was apparent to most of us that some form of specialization was going to be necessary if we were to make any sort of living off our holdings. We knew families who were already claiming to be self-sufficient, but it simply wasn't true. Some were receiving State or ex-company pensions, some took in paying guests, and others' idea of 'a living' was not much more than a hillbilly existence. But the wealth of ideas put before us by the horticultural lecturers opened our eyes to new possibilities.

'The housewife,' we learned, 'will pay a lot for out-of-season vegetables...'

'Silly cow,' someone muttered, scribbling away in her notebook.

'...as much as £1 a pound for early runner beans.' The lecturer paused and grinned at the sea of incredulous faces before him. Pens raced over paper, you could almost see £ signs in bubbles poised over everyone's head. *Runner beans?* The crop you tried to *give* away in September?

'Early cauliflowers,' continued the expert, 'lettuce, courgettes, even rhubarb, make high prices if you can market them early enough.' He went on to list other salad and vegetable varieties that this demented housewife couldn't wait to get her hands on. We had met her before, of course, at last year's lectures on animal husbandry. She was the one who didn't like fat on her beef and couldn't tell a battery egg from a real one. And now here she was, forking out £1 a pound for runners.

Our fantasy that we could all be rich, would one day be able to buy clothes at Marks instead of Oxfam, was fleeting. Having whetted our appetites for the end product, the lecturer now brought us down to earth. Soil sterilization, seed tray sterilization, fumigation of the growing area...crumbs, I thought, all that washing-up before you've even planted a seed. Then, using lettuce as an example, we learned what a young seedling can expect after it has surfaced through the decontaminated growing medium into the decontaminated and expensively heated air of the commercial glasshouse.

Slugs, for a start, then weevils, aphids and the like (quite how they survived all the pre-washing-up I'm not sure), all sucking away at lettuce sap and transmitting viruses. Miraculously, and with the help of some expensive sprays, your young lettuce shrugs off these childhood ailments and stretches its legs down into the soil. If you have got your irrigation and drainage right, all will be well, but if you haven't, the lettuce will get a sort of athlete's foot called botrytis.

The hazards seemed to be endless. How did a commercial grower ever get a night's sleep with such battles raging in his greenhouse? There were human pests to contend with too, lettuce thieves no less. (*Lettuce thieves?*) Small wonder that out-of-season glasshouse crops were so expensive.

After the coffee break, we saw some slides of forced rhubarb, and our hopes rose again. Rhubarb has only one enemy – the black bean aphid – and even that seemed to be an amateur compared to the anti-lettuce brigade. But nobody ever got into the supertax bracket on rhubarb. Commercial horticulture seemed like everything else in life – a matter of getting out what you were prepared to put in. Anyone sinking their savings into glasshouses and modern equipment could do well, but it was a gamble. Another Middle East crisis and the price of oil might rise so high as to make even 'the housewife' think twice before buying a winter lettuce.

'I shall stick to calves,' said a friend called Chris, when the lecture was over and some of us were making for the pub over the road. 'All this Percy Thrower stuff would give me ulcers if my livelihood depended on it.'

'Perhaps the teachers are showing us the worst side first?' suggested Brian. 'At the start of the animal husbandry course it seemed the same. I haven't recovered from those tapeworm slides yet, but I've never seen an actual tapeworm.'

'Haven't you really?' said another friend. 'I bought a couple of gilts recently and one of them had a whopper. We had to grab hold of one end of it and walk her forwards to –'

'Do you *mind*,' said someone crossly. 'I'm just about to have a pork pie with my beer.'

When Parsley's puppies were ten weeks old, Leoni came round for a final assessment of them before we advertised them for sale. They raced round the garden with Ella, who had taken charge of them as soon as Parsley had lost interest some two or three weeks previously.

'Marvellous litter,' said Leoni. 'What have you reared them on?'

'Jersey milk and rabbit mainly. Milk and wholewheat cereals for their morning feeds, and raw rabbit with cooked carrot for the others. Oh, and cod liver oil and seaweed supplements.'

'You're going to have a job to find owners who can keep that up. Rabbit is 80 pence a pound in Sainsbury's.'

'They can be switched to heart or cheap beef now,' I said. 'It's only because I've got plenty of surplus rabbit that they've had so much.' Rabbit wholesalers were paying 32 pence a pound at that time, about the same as I would have had to pay for ox heart or offal, so it came to the same thing. Actually, I don't think it matters much what the meat is as long as it isn't tinned.

Leoni arranged for a friend of hers who wanted a dual-purpose dog (pet and show) to come and have the pick of the litter. This was still Teazel, although why one puppy should stand out is hard to explain. It's a combination of shape, markings and that indefinable something, which is called star quality in humans. In dogs it has a lot to do with head carriage – a sort of 'look at me, I'm the greatest' bearing, with the crest of the neck arched like a stallion.

When Leoni's friend arrived, Teazel had just finished showing the other puppies how to explore a drain. They had somehow managed to dislodge the metal grating over a 4-inch soakaway pipe and their heads and front paws were green with slime.

'Oh, you beauty,' enthused the prospective buyer, swooping Teazel plus effluent into her arms. It confirmed my opinion that all dog lovers – including self – are potty. (It also reminded me of the time I had gone to collect Parsley. Knowing nothing about pedigree dogs, I had been struck dumb when the breeder, holding the infant Parsley in her cupped hands, said seriously, 'It's dogs like this that make me want to get back in the ring.')

After Teazel had gone, I wiped my eyes and phoned an advert in to the local paper. A week later all the puppies had gone – to *kind*, *good* homes I had to keep telling myself every time I passed an abandoned bone still etched with tiny tooth-marks. The puppy buyers had been really nice people, all experienced dog owners. One stout, jolly lady, a sub-postmistress with red marks on her shoulders where her dress straps cut in, had sunk into an armchair and waited to be 'chosen' by one of the puppies. To my delight, Fatty had been the first to settle down in the accommodating lap.

'What's her name?' asked the postmistress.

I reeled off Fatty's long Kennel Club-registered name, full of prefixes and suffixes.

'Goodness, what a mouthful. I shall call her Podge.'

And I, blinking back the tears as Fatty/Podge was borne away, squashed into the bosom of her new owner, couldn't help laughing. The postmistress had ordered a 'Beware of the Dog' sign for the shop door.

I don't like all dogs, though, nor all dog owners. My *bête noire* is uncastrated dogs, particularly those with owners who say gaily, 'Oh, he's only marking his territory,' when hot, un-diluted urine cascades over our garden plants. In vain have we pointed out that it's *our* territory that's being marked. One cock of the leg, and a tubful of geraniums – at 50 pence each – is ruined. I get mad and, like the Red Queen in reverse, want to order certain bits to be chopped off. 'Castration is unnatural,' say these morons, conveniently forgetting that cats, sheep, bulls and horses are routinely castrated.

The topic arose when Sara and Gerry came to stay for Christmas. Dylan, one of their spaniels, was fully grown now, but as there were no geraniums for him to defoliate, we managed to keep the question of neutering fairly amicable. In any case, the weather was so cold that none of the dogs stayed outside very long. All seven of them liked to huddle round Anne's log fire, which was a very good thing as far as I was concerned because it kept Gilbert spider at bay beneath the log pile. I had tried to murder Gilbert once by hoovering him up when he strolled into our part of the house, but Anne had emptied the dust bag on to a piece of newspaper and rescued him, still alive unfortunately. She wouldn't speak to me for a whole day. Marcus, when he heard of the incident, sent us a funny cartoon-like drawing of Gilbert on crutches with some of his legs in plaster.

One evening, Brian and I took Sara and Gerry to visit some friends of ours, Rob and Chris, who lived about 12 miles away. 'You'd better come early,' Rob said. 'The weather forecast was bad, so you might have to leave early.' Gerry's borrowed Land Rover was low on diesel, so we went in the Transit van, slipping and sliding on the ice in the narrow lanes.

No sooner had we all settled down in front of the fire with glasses of plonk, than it started to snow. 'Oh, *no*,' we groaned. 'Surely we had enough last year to last a lifetime?'

'Let's stay a bit longer,' Sara pleaded. 'It doesn't look too bad.' She had made friends with Chris and Rob's deer-hound and was loath to go.

'We'll give it half an hour,' said Brian. 'But we're a long way from home and we don't want to be stranded here.'

'No, you don't,' agreed Chris. Their cottage was tiny and Chris was heavily pregnant with their first son. (We knew it was a son because she and I had 'dowsed' her abdomen with a darning needle on a piece of cotton, an infallible method of sexing the unborn, even with dogs if you can work out which way the puppies are lying.) 'You can sleep in the barn if you don't mind sharing with sheep,' she offered.

'Oh, you've brought them in then?' I said. 'Do you think it's really going to be as bad as last year?'

Chris shook her head. 'I don't think we'll ever see snow like that again,' she said. 'But we're not taking any chances. By the way, can I borrow Ramrod for my ewes soon?'

'Ramrod?' I said in surprise. 'Yes, of course you can, but he's not proven yet. He's supposed to be serving our Jacobs at the moment but he hasn't shown the slightest interest in them.'

'Sensible fellow,' said Rob, who had been roped in to help with our sheep-dipping earlier in the year. He was one of the calmest people we knew, but even he had been driven to suggest to the dipping attendant that a two-hour total immersion of certain woolly creatures might solve a lot of problems.

'I thought you were going to borrow Boaz?' said Brian.

'Jayne's ram? Yes, we were, but he's booked right up until March. We thought we might try Ramrod first, then use Boaz on any that Ramrod misses.'

We chatted until nine o'clock, then decided to leave as the snow was still falling. The Transit wheels spun a little at first, but it soon gained momentum and carried us somewhat skiddily for about 6 miles. But then we found the ridge road along the top of the Blackdown Hills was virtually impassable. High winds had whipped the snow into drifts and you couldn't see which was road and which was ditch. 'Oops,' Brian muttered as the van waltzed sideways. The engine cut out.

'I think we're in a ditch, Brian,' said Sara.

'I had worked that out, thank you. I don't drive at an angle of 45 degrees as a rule.'

We climbed out and attacked the snow in the ditch with spades. ('I'm sure we never used to take spades when we dined out in London,' Brian complained.) The wind stung our eyes and blew the falling snow inside our anorak hoods. We couldn't shift the van and were just about to abandon it and start walking when we heard an engine labouring up the hill behind us. Soon a bright fog-light appeared and then, incredibly, a *snow-plough*.

'I do believe in fairies,' said Brian piously. He waved the driver down and explained our plight. The cheery driver, who had some terrible Radio 1 music blaring out of the cab, hitched a rope to the back of his machine and pulled the van out of the ditch as easily as popping a cork. We were able to follow in the snow-plough's tracks for almost 3 miles before our routes diverged. We had to make a steep descent from the ridge road, and one look at the state of our turn-off road decided Brian. 'We'll park somewhere safe and walk,' he said. 'It's only a couple of miles now.'

The rest of the journey was horrible. The wind, which we learned the next day had reached blizzard proportions while we were out in it, ripped and tugged at our clothes and drove needles of ice into our faces. Snow drifts now approaching several feet in exposed places caught us unawares – we only had one torch between us – but the worst thing was the noise, the endless wind that a wet anorak hood couldn't keep out. It was after midnight when four exhausted bedraggled creatures dripped into the house. 'Anne must be so worried,' said Sara. 'I'll go and tell her we're OK.'

Anne was watching the late-night horror film. 'Worried?' she said. 'Why should I be worried?'

'Because we've been up to our necks – well, waists – in *snow*. There's a gale out there, it's pitch dark and we've been blown about like leaves.'

'I've been watching *The Hairy Hand*,' said Anne, as if that excused her from worrying. 'It was supposed to be frightening.'

'We saw *The Hairy Hand* ages ago,' said Gerry. 'It was rubbish.'

'Yes, it was,' Anne agreed. Then she noticed our wet clothes. 'As you're wet already,' she said, 'would one of you mind taking the dogs out? The weather forecast wasn't too good for tonight.'

The 1979 snow – the Big Freeze, as the media called it – brought most parts of Britain to a halt for anything up to several weeks. The snow came in two waves, the first falling on 1 January (the night we were out in it) and lying a few days, then the really heavy fall on 17 January. In between these dates, most roads, though icy, were passable, and Sara and Gerry returned to their job in Sussex.

After they had gone, Brian and I tried to get round to as many of our smallholding friends as possible to help them to prepare for the next snow that had been forecast. Our own stock was safely under cover. Every animal (except the Jacobs, which we couldn't catch) and bird was penned with its own store of feed placed nearby to avoid a repetition of last year's nightmare feeding rounds. Most of our friends had space problems – lack of it, that is – and we helped to remove cars from garages, junk from disused outside lavatories and even, in one case, furniture from a conservatory. Then straw was humped in and plastic feed bins, with elastic straps stretched from handle to handle to stop the animals from helping themselves, placed within easy reach. It was like preparing for war, using hay and straw bales instead of sandbags.

Blizzards raged along the east coast of America, and everyone knew it wouldn't be long before it was Britain's turn. There was nothing we could do except wait quietly and hope that moorland farmers would show some compassion for their outwintered animals and get them on to lower ground. (They didn't, of course. Even with three weeks' advance snow warning, they didn't. Cushioned by ministry grants, subsidies and compensations, why should they?)

A few days after Sara and Gerry had gone, they unexpectedly came back, their old banger piled high with all their worldly goods. 'Oh, no,' we groaned.

'It's not for long,' they said, sensing that they were not getting the red-carpet treatment. 'Just until we find another job.' A few minor disagreements with their employer had suddenly erupted into a full-scale row. Neither side would see the other's point of view, so Sara and Gerry had packed their bags and walked out.

Hearing voices in the yard, Anne came out. 'Ruffin, Dylan – how nice. Hello, kids. Are you having another holiday?'

'It's not a holiday,' I said coldly. 'They've given up their job.'

Anne said kindly, 'Never mind. You'll soon get another one. Bring the dogs in and I'll put the kettle on.' She went indoors and Brian and I helped to unload the car. Sara said she thought grandmothers were nature's way of preventing parents and children actually injuring each other. 'Like train buffers,' she said. 'You and Brian were just going to start lecturing us about irresponsibility, weren't you?'

'It won't stop us,' Brian said. 'You've made yourselves homeless, jobless and probably penniless. You'll get the lecture later.'

Sara and Gerry took their luggage upstairs. Brian and I went to have a pow-wow with Anne. 'She doesn't change, does she?' said Anne. 'Sara, I mean. So *impetuous*. Do you remember when she kept running away from home?'

Yes, I remembered. How embarrassing it had been. Sara was

three and a half, and instead of running away somewhere interesting, like to join a circus, she had repeatedly run away to school. She thought Marcus was having all the fun while she was stuck at home with me and *Listen with Mother*. The headmistress had found it very amusing, and in the face of such determination, had felt obliged to offer Sara a place in the reception class.

As the weather worsened, we all shelved the youngsters' future job problems and settled down for the siege. When the snow came, we dutifully got the camera out and, with a feeling of *déjà vu*, tunnelled out of the garden and walked over the gate.

Chapter Twenty

The snow differed from last year's: it was hard and froze solid as soon as it landed so that, although the drifts were immense in places, you could walk over them without sinking up to your head. The air was achingly cold, the sort of weather where you didn't dare to touch anything metal with your bare hands or you would be likely to stick to it.

Each day we put a bale of hay on a sledge and hauled it up to the sheep's field. Normally, the 12-foot hedges kept them in, but once the drifting snow had provided them with a gigantic stepping-stone, they were over and gone. The first time this happened, an irate landowner some 2 miles away phoned up and demanded we come and 'remove your flaming sheep from my property'. He had formal lawns, but since these were a couple of feet under snow, it seemed highly unlikely that the Jacobs were doing them any harm.

However, wishing to keep the peace and with a sneaking sympathy for anybody who wished to see the back of Jacobs, we floundered over to fetch them. Directly we got them home – an unforgettable march along blocked lanes, which took half a day – they escaped, in a different direction this time, so we gave up. The next day their bale of hay had been eaten. This pattern continued throughout the freeze-up: the Jacobs kangarood around the countryside, returning home once a day to eat their hay.

Another escapee was Ramrod's friend, Hamish. A woman phoned at ten o'clock one evening and asked if we had lost a large white rabbit, as she and her husband had found one in their garden. They had only recently moved into the area, but had heard that we kept rabbits.

When Brian and I went to count our lot (they were temporarily in hutches in a barn for convenience), we found that Hamish's door was open and the hutch empty.

'Look,' I said, shining a torch on the snow outside the barn, 'there are his footprints.' We followed his hop-marks for about 200 yards along the road to where the young couple lived. Their cottage was a converted old forge, very picturesque and cosy. Even cosier was the scene inside. Hamish was sitting up on their settee eating a bag of crisps and having his back stroked. 'He followed me in when I called him,' the girl said. 'I couldn't believe it.'

They brushed aside our apologies for the gatecrasher and invited us to stay and have some coffee. They were very taken with Hamish and wanted to know how he came to be out on his own in the dark. We explained how we normally kept the rabbits in a large shed, but because of the bitter weather had put them in hutches which were warmer. 'I must have forgotten to shut Hamish's,' I said, 'but I wouldn't have thought he could have got so far in the snow.'

Hamish lost interest in his crisps when he saw biscuits being handed round with coffee. For a rabbit, he was quite a good guest, not making too many crumbs. After he had eaten, he washed his ears, pulling them down over his face with his paws. Then he hopped off the settee and went over to investigate a wicker log basket in the fireplace. 'I think we'd better take him home before he starts gnawing things,' said Brian. 'Thanks very much for looking after him and for the coffee.'

The young couple saw us to the door and insisted on giving Hamish the rest of the crisps to take home. 'You mustn't spoil him,' we laughed. 'He might tell the others and you'll have them all queuing up outside your door.'

The snow lay for three weeks in the West Country, and much longer in some other regions. The thaw brought nation-wide flooding and terrible hardship to farm stock and humans. Some friends of ours in the 'wetlands' of Sedgmoor had their house and buildings flooded to a depth of nearly 3 feet and had to use a rowing boat to get to the shops. Every night the TV news told the same tragic stories: drowned animals, homeless people and ruined property.

Our lamb-bank friend Betty had a heartening story to tell. Near her lived a family whose house was built below the level of a main road and which had been flooded in the previous year's thaw. This year Betty's resourceful fifteen-year-old daughter, Erika, had thought up a brilliant way of diverting the flood water. Taking her metal-detector out on to the thick snow in the main road, Erika had cast about until she located the manhole nearest to the endangered house. She dug down to the manhole and removed the cover. When the snow melted, most of it whooshed down the huge drain and the occupants of the house were able to keep the remainder out with sandbags.

As soon as the roads in the southern half of England were passable again, Sara and Gerry started job-hunting. Marcus wanted them to join him on the permanent staff of PGC, the children's holiday centre in Brecon, but they weren't keen. They had both enjoyed the independence of their warden-cum-caretaking job and were looking for something similar. Their ex-employer wanted them back, and when they declined, was still decent enough to give them glowing references.

They advertised themselves in the 'Situations Wanted' columns of several glossy magazines and were flooded with replies. These ranged from people who offered chauffeur/nanny posts, to impoverished pensioners who needed someone to cut their hedges and lawns regularly. Some of the in-between ones sounded promising, and the kids, armed with their references, started doing the rounds of prospective employers. They travelled to crumbling stately homes whose grounds had not had a sighting of shears for decades, and to pop stars' country retreats lavish in spending and low on taste. Some of the would-be employers were nice, some nasty and some plain batty.

One of the battier ones was an elderly widow who kept goats. The job sounded all right in her letter: a beautiful old house in the Cotswolds with a self-contained staff cottage, duties to include complete charge of 15 acres and some help with the goats. What was *not* mentioned was that already in the staff cottage was an ancient drunk called Ernest who, as Sara put it, 'sort of went with the job'.

'But who *was* Ernest?' we asked, trying to picture the scene from Sara's and Gerry's somewhat garbled account of the interview.

'That was the funniest thing,' Sara giggled. 'The old lady

didn't seem to know who he was. When she opened the door of the staff cottage to show us round there was this smelly old bundle spark out on the floor. She said, 'You mustn't mind Ernest,' and just stepped over him.

'She was amazingly vague,' Gerry added. 'She said Ernest had "always" been there. She didn't remember if he was a relation of her husband's or an old servant or what. When we asked if there was any other place he could go, she wouldn't hear of it, said it would be too upsetting for him.'

'She gives him a hot meal in her own house once a day,' Sara continued. 'He spends his pension on cider and sleeps it off in the cottage. She kept repeating that she couldn't keep staff for five minutes and sounding *surprised* about it!'

Sara and Gerry decided that £100 a week plus cottage, which was generous by normal standards, was not really enough to overlook the presence of Ernest. 'Pity though,' Gerry said reflectively. 'There was some good game fishing in the valley.'

They continued their job hunt. Brian and I set to work to make good the damage done by the blizzards, and Anne, full of pent-up energy after being snow-bound for three weeks, went out and bought herself a car.

The dealer who delivered it handed Brian the log book and keys, a chauvinistic gesture that would normally have enraged Anne, but she was so excited about the car she didn't notice. 'I've remembered to buy L plates,' she said. 'Now, who's going to be first to come for a drive with me?'

After a long silence I said, 'We all will.'

'Do you believe in safety in numbers or something?' Sara whispered as she, Gerry and I took the back seat with Brian monitoring Anne from the passenger seat.

Brian showed Anne what all the controls were for, laying particular emphasis on the foot brake. Then he suggested that she drive slowly towards the gateway and stop. She switched the ignition on and engaged the gear, which was automatic.

The car slid forwards smoothly, down the drive, straight through the gateway, out on to the road and away.

'What are you all shouting for?' she said crossly. 'It's easy. The dealer said automatics are child's play.'

'The *brake*,' Brian gasped. 'I told you to put your foot on the brake when we got to the gate. Will you please *stop*.'

It was all too much like her ride on Wellington with me. As soon as the car was stationary (in the middle of the road) I opened my door and made my getaway. 'I'll walk home,' I said to Brian.

'Me too,' said Sara, scrambling out after me. Gerry nobly stayed to give Brian much-needed moral support.

'Do you think she didn't hear Brian telling her to stop at the gate?' Sara asked.

'She heard all right. She had no intention of tamely driving up and down the yard for her first lesson.'

'She's awfully brave, isn't she? I'm surprised they give driving licences to pensioners actually. I mean the roads are –'

'Licence!' I said suddenly. 'Oh, heck, I bet she's forgotten to buy a provisional one.'

'Licence? Of course I bought a licence,' said Anne later, when everyone was on speaking terms again. 'Although with such a feeble family I don't suppose I'll be allowed to drive my own car again.' She was still a bit put out at being ordered to change places with Brian after she had shot round a round-about without slowing down. Brian and Gerry, both non-spirit drinkers, had felt drawn to the idea of a small brandy after their outing.

'You'll have to have proper lessons at a driving school,' Brian said. 'I'm sorry, but I can't afford to be injured at the moment.'

'It's your reaction time, Anne,' Gerry explained. 'If Brian says slow down and apply the brake, he means *now* – not after you've spent a minute thinking about it.'

Reluctantly, Anne agreed to book herself six driving lessons from a school in Taunton. 'Perhaps you would take me out for some practice in between lessons, Gerry?' she said hopefully. 'You're better at explaining things than Brian.'

'He's got younger nerves,' said Brian snappily, and went off to sort out his seed potatoes for chitting.

We went to a smallholders' meeting that evening. It was given by the National Trust and the lecture was entitled 'The

Conservation of our Countryside'. Anne's progress along the main road to Taunton earlier in the day had not gone unnoticed by some of our local friends and Brian came in for a lot of ribbing about 'the destruction of our countryside' by throttle-happy mothers-in-law.

The lecture was one of the most interesting the SHA had had. We were shown how to work out the ages of hedgerows and pastures by noting the different sorts of plants growing in them. There were certain plants, such as hemlock, forget-me-not and yellow rattle, that grew wild only in fields that had not been ploughed for hundreds of years, and when Brian and I saw slides of these, we recognized all three as species that grew abundantly in our hayfield. The lecturer, who was a young woman with an infectious enthusiasm for her subject, unconsciously raised a big laugh when she begged us all to leave 'wild' areas on our holdings: areas of nettles for butterflies to breed in, bogs for damp-loving flora and fauna, and uncut hedges for small mammals and birds. Even if we had wanted to, there wasn't a member present who could afford the machinery to drain bogs or grub hedges.

As spring approached, Brian drew up a master plan for the coming year. To my relief he decided not to plant any more anemones – we had picked the last 140 bunches in late December before a hard frost brought merciful release – but estimated that the one-year-old corms would yield a reduced crop that we could cope with. (He failed to reckon the energizing qualities of well-rotted farmyard manure.) He would make better use of the polytunnel to grow early cash crops, and might even buy another one after the Horticultural Course had finished. He would work harder. Strewth! I must work harder. Strewth again! The ponies must put in a longer working day. Now that I had Sarah B to call on during holidays and weekends, I must not turn away any customers for trivial reasons.

'*Trivial?*' I cut in. 'If you're referring to that awful Morgan man who talks in parables, I don't call him trivial. He's ghastly and his kids pick their noses.'

'I thought he talked in clichés,' Brian said. 'The first time he cornered me I got a lecture on "When one door closes another one opens".'

'I remember,' I giggled. Mr Morgan, a layabout with a hard-working wife, was one of the crashingest bores we had ever encountered. He spent his entire life seeing 'messages' in commonplace events. Pigeons, for instance, were never pigeons. They were doves or omens of peace. The fact that they stripped the peas and crapped everywhere didn't bother Morgan because he was too lazy to grow peas and too self-centred to notice mess.

'OK, I give in over Morgan,' Brian said. 'Only when he phones up, don't expect me to say that you're booked for the next six Saturdays.' He consulted his notes again. 'More growing, more riding and more calves. Same number of pigs?'

'Yes. Six is about right.' There's a saying that people keep pigs for two reasons only – muck and company. It's a very old saying, which seems to indicate that there has never been much profit in pigs.

'Sheep,' Brian continued with relish. The time had come to advertise the Jacobs. Ramrod had run with them for over two months, so they ought to be pregnant. We would ask a pregnant price for them and if any failed to produce a lamb we would reimburse the new owners the difference. Phoning the advert in to a not-too-local paper was a great pleasure. Before the paper came out, we sold Cleo to a local friend who had tame ewes. She would become lonely without the company of a flock. Ramrod was still on loan to Chris and Rob, and booked for a further month to other smallholding friends. We could decide what to do with him later in the year, but as he still preferred humans to sheep, it wasn't really a problem.

Three separate people bought the six Jacob ewes and their four yearling ewe lambs. We got £265 for the adults and £15 each for the lambs and felt we had earned every farthing. Twenty-four hours after they had gone, two came back. They had travelled about 7 miles and had crossed a main road on the way. Mr Morgan would undoubtedly have found something symbolic about our sheep returning to the fold, but we viewed them in quite a different light. Would we never be rid of the pests? We phoned the new owner, who *apologized* for letting them stray.

After the usual undignified chase and capture, Brian redelivered them and waited until he had seen them put into goat collars at the end of long chains fastened to apple trees. They bucketed around until they had knocked off the last of their fresh horn growth, then they gave in. Of the others, one group gave no trouble at all, while the third continued to hedge-hop until they lambed in late spring.

Sara and Gerry, still jobless, were now beginning to find that there wasn't really enough room in the house for three generations plus dogs. They had a lot of luggage, and the spare rooms were already full of stored furniture and overwintering geraniums and fuchsias. 'There'll always be a home for you here if you really need it,' we told them as we carried trays of chitting potatoes into their bedroom.

They took the hint and moved out a few days later. Lin and John had offered them the empty chalet at Phyllishayes until it was needed for holiday guests later on. It was a most convenient arrangement all round, not least for us, as the amount of mud carried into the house by two large spaniels is out of all proportion to the number of paws they have.

On the days when they weren't job-hunting, Sara helped me with the riding lessons, which were beginning to pick up again as snowdrops and primroses enticed parents of pony-loving children out of their houses. Our place was quite well situated for parents to enjoy an hour's stroll in the woods while their children rode.

One couple, carrying some professional-looking photographic gear, got quite worked up about the scenery, and took dozens of pictures in the Blackdowns, while Sara and I took their two children riding. I don't know who they were or if there was any connection, but not long afterwards, the place they had photographed most was designated an area of outstanding natural beauty and now enjoys official protection.

The children of this couple were called Mervyn and Megan and were the most entertaining kids Sara and I had come across for a long while. Mervyn was nine and a half and Megan eight. They both used words so precisely that you felt you knew the people they were describing. For instance, Mervyn, describing a tiresome aunt, said 'she pushes my hair about', which, if you think about it, is exactly what tiresome aunts do. A grown-up would probably say 'rumples' or 'ruffles', but a small boy knows what it feels like from underneath.

One of their pets was a failed goldfish. Sara had asked Megan if they had any pets and Megan said: 'Oh, yes. A dog and two cats and a failed goldfish.'

'A failed goldfish?' I said intrigued.

Goldie was just no good at being a goldfish, they explained. 'He jumped out of his tank when we first had him,' Mervyn said. 'Daddy had to fix a net over the top. He's bored being a fish. He keeps biting the glass to get out. Megan and I think he wants to be a crocodile.'

'We know a boy called Hugh,' continued Megan. 'He's just like Goldie. His parents are vegetarians but he's not.'

'I'm sorry to be so dim, Megan,' I said, 'but I'm afraid you've lost me. What have Hugh's parents got to do with Goldie?'

Megan said patiently: 'Hugh couldn't talk when he was a baby, could he? He had to put up with nasty beans and hard pastry until he could talk. Imagine having to wait all that time before you could have a proper dinner.'

'I see,' I said. 'So you think Goldie's trying to tell you something when he bites the glass?'

'We're sure he is,' said Mervyn. 'We took him to the vet's in a bucket. The vet said perhaps he'd be happier in a garden pond.' They chatted on and on, a charming pair of budding naturalists. They were going to join Frog Watch this year, they told us, and fill in forms to send to the Nature Conservancy Council. It bore out my theory that Frog Watch is not so much a way of finding frogs as finding colonies of middle-class, literate children with an interest in natural history.

'Weren't they terrific?' Sara said after they had gone. 'I must tell Marcus about the nasty beans and the hard pastry. He could use it as a title for a vegetarian cookery book.'

'A failed cookery book?'

If smallholders could have one wish, I guess it would be something connected with weather. Just the smallest peek into the future would do; just enough to stop soft-fruit growers from losing their crops in June storms, or to warn suckler-herd owners that there would be no grazing in August because a drought was on the way.

Forewarned, we might have made different plans for 1979. But not knowing that it was going to be the coldest, wettest three months in over 100 years (Wimbledon was actually postponed), we and our fellow smallholders planned the year on a business-as-usual basis.

There was a lot to look forward to. After the Horticultural Course, there would be the SHA's own programme of lectures, demonstrations, outings and practical work. Ideas would be discussed for small, specialist crops: teasels for the weaving industry, ornamental grasses and gourds for the Christmas trade, woad for dyers. The woad talk was going to be particularly popular: even in committee, we couldn't resist pushing the boat out with references to 'woad accidents', 'the woad to wuin' and so on. In high summer there was going to be a day-long demonstration of haymaking the Swiss way – on cocked ash-pole tripods with vents left in the hay walls to ensure a long, slow drying. Stalls were booked for the Honiton and Dunster shows; a date fixed for wassailing an orchard in late autumn...

'I don't know how you're going to fit it all in,' said Addy, studying the calendar on the kitchen wall. It was March and Addy had just arrived for a week's stay. The coach bringing her from Kent to Devon had been late. 'Didn't stop raining all the way,' she said, hanging up her coat behind the door. 'Is Anne in?'

'No. She won't be long, though,' I said. 'She's having a driving lesson.' Her third, with three different instructors. She had not yet grasped the implication of this, and continued to zoom around Taunton as if it were Brands Hatch.

Addy stooped to stroke Honey, who was tucked up in her basket with a hot-water bottle. 'Hello, my old darling. What's the matter with you?'

'She's a bit off colour,' Brian said quickly. The truth was that Honey was quietly and peacefully dying. We would tell Addy later, not now when she was tired from her long trip.

Three days previously, Honey, at thirteen and a half, had climbed stiffly into her basket and settled down to wait for death. It was sad but inevitable, as every pet owner knows. I tried to tempt her appetite with every conceivable delicacy, but she refused all solids. Five times a day I spooned glucose and water down her throat and carried her outside to pee. Her temperature and pulse were normal and she was in no pain.

'Off colour?' said Addy. 'Have you called the vet?'

Brian and I looked at each other. Addy would have to be told. 'She's old, Mum,' Brian said. 'She's ninety-one in human years. It wouldn't be fair to keep her going with injections and drugs if she's had enough. We want her to die in peace.'

'She's not going to die,' said Addy briskly. 'I know what she needs – a cup of tea.'

Now that we had a working knowledge of animal husbandry, parasitology, bacteriology and veterinary first aid, we knew that Addy's quaint notion wouldn't do any harm. A cup of tea would give Honey a change of flavour after glucose and water.

Addy made a pot of very strong tea – I think she used six spoonfuls to a pint of water – and added milk and sugar. When it was cool enough, she sat Honey up and coaxed her to drink about half.

An hour later Honey needed to go outside. I buckled her coat round her and carried her to the end of the garden, where she did a huge puddle. Instead of letting me carry her indoors again, she walked, rather unsteadily but with a definite purpose. Addy repeated the strong tea treatment.

By suppertime Honey's eyes had brightened and she managed a feeble thump of her tail when she saw the other dogs having their dinners. By morning, she was on an invalid diet of chicken and baby cereal, and from that day to the day she actually died, at the age of sixteen and a half, she was never ill again.

'You see, Honey,' Addy said to her, 'you've got to face facts. They're short-handed here. Nobody's allowed to leave just because they're ninety-one.'

Other books in the series:

The Year of the Cornflake by Faith Addis

After finding the house of their dreams and undertaking an air-born race to make sure they get it, Faith and Brian discover that the hard work begins. Overhauling the house, buying live-stock they know nothing about and recapturing escaped horses all try the family's patience. And when children start arriving for the children's holiday venture Faith and Brian know their work's going to be cut out ....

Green Behind the Ears by Faith Addis

Phillishayes Children's Holidays is established, and Faith and Brian are settling down for the winter after a frenetic summer of holidaying children. A minor upset with a dog giving birth to puppies under the house and a serious scare when Marcus is hurt in a road accident set the scene as Faith, Brian and the rest of the Addis family continue to settle into rural Devonshire life in the second instalment of the *Down to Earth* series.

It's Better than Work by Faith Addis

Faith is back in London learning the delicate art of dog grooming, while Brian insists on getting his and the dog's frozen food mixed up. In Devon Faith and Brian launch their next venture: a nursery and market garden. Once up and running they have to deal with the eccentric customers that come by, including a TV crew searching for daffodils in August! In the fourth instalment of the *Down to Earth* series Faith once again proves that life in Devon is never dull.

Taking the Biscuit by Faith Addis

A gift of 800 worms isn't to everyone's taste, but Faith is delighted and plans to become Devon's first worm tycoon. Meanwhile Brian, in a government youth motivating programme, is ferrying a bunch of Totnes' young bohemians around the countryside charting the local by-ways. Add to this Faith's very conservative dog-grooming customers and her irrepressible mother's love of Totnes and *Taking the Biscuit* does exactly what its title suggests in the final instalment of the *Down to Earth* series.